WAL

WALKING WITH THE BRONTËS
IN WEST YORKSHIRE

F
FRANCES LINCOLN LIMITED
PUBLISHERS

Frances Lincoln Limited
4 Torriano Mews
Torriano Avenue
London NW5 2RZ
www.franceslincoln.com

Walking with the Brontës
Copyright © Frances Lincoln
Limited 2012
Text and photographs copyright
© Norman and June Buckley 2012
with the exception of the
photographs on pages 1, 12, 46,
54–5, 62, 70 and 88, which are
copyright © Simon Warner
Illustrated maps copyright
© Martin Ursell
First Frances Lincoln edition 2012

A catalogue record for this book is
available from the British Library.

978-0-7112-3254-9

Printed and bound in China

1 2 3 4 5 6 7 8 9

Page 1: Landscape near Thornton,
Bradford.
Pages 2–3: River Aire near Apperley
Bridge.
Right: South Dean Brook, near
Brontë Bridge, Haworth Moor.

CONTENTS

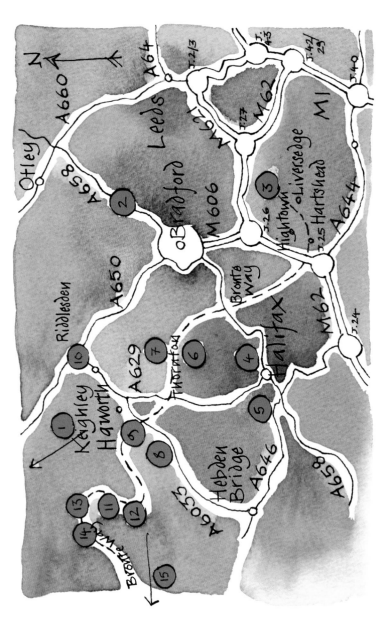

INTRODUCTION

The fifteen walks included in this book are mainly but not wholly located in West Yorkshire. This area includes the conurbations of Leeds and Bradford and encompasses large swathes of former industrial activity, small towns and villages often merging across a hard countryside dotted with isolated stone-built farmhouses and scarred by former mines and quarries. The western side rises to high moorland, which is bleak and frequently windswept but of compelling attraction to generations of walkers; this is where the Pennines separate the counties of Lancashire and Yorkshire. The part of the area, including moors, which is close to Haworth is known as 'Brontë Country'.

The selection of the routes in this book is, inevitably, dictated by the presence of the Brontë family in West Yorkshire and adjacent Lancashire, their homes, their places of education, their workplaces and the buildings and landscape which so influenced the content of their novels. In order to facilitate maximum accessibility, the walks are predominantly short and none is difficult or unduly demanding. Every walk has some connection with one or more members of the family. At the eastern end of the area is 'Shirley Country', so called because it provided the setting for Charlotte Brontë's novel *Shirley*. Threading its way from Oakwell Hall, to the south of Bradford, in Shirley Country to Gawthorpe Hall, near Burnley, is the Brontë Way, a continuous footpath 67.5km (42 miles) long linking many of the sites associated with the family. Several lengths of this are included in the walks here. When walking along the Way and, perhaps, even more so when crossing Haworth and Stanbury Moors, the Brontë sisters' love of wild places so fundamental to their spirit and which so influenced their writing will be readily apparent.

THE BRONTË FAMILY

The Brontë story begins in Ireland on 17 March 1777, when Patrick Brontë (then Brunty) was born, the eldest of ten children of a peasant farmer. After short spells apprenticed to a blacksmith, as a linen weaver and then as a teacher, Patrick was engaged as a tutor by the Vicar of Drumgooland. Recognizing his potential, the vicar was instrumental in obtaining Patrick's admission to St John's College, Cambridge, in September 1802. Patrick soon changed his surname to Bronte, adding the accent on the 'e' later. He graduated with a Bachelor of Arts degree in April 1806, and was ordained in August of the same year.

After short spells in posts at Cambridge, Wethersfield (Essex) and Wellington (Shropshire), in December 1809 Patrick arrived in Dewsbury as curate at the parish church. So began his long ministry to the people of West Yorkshire. His next post was at nearby Hartshead, where he was inducted in July 1811. After a brief courtship he married Maria Branwell, a Cornish girl, at Guiseley Parish Church, near Leeds, on 29 December 1812.

The Brontës set up house at Clough Lane, Hightown, not far from Hartshead. Children arrived with great frequency. Maria was born in January 1814 and Elizabeth in February 1815, both at Hightown. In March 1815 Patrick exchanged the living of Hartshead for that of Thornton, near Bradford. Charlotte, April 1816, Patrick Branwell, June 1817, Emily Jane, July 1818, and Anne, January 1820, were all born at the Vicarage, 74 Market Street, Thornton, completing the family. In April 1820 the family moved to the Parsonage, Haworth, Patrick having secured the perpetual curacy of St Michael and All Angels.

The prolonged family tragedy was soon to begin: within eighteen months Patrick's wife had died of cancer, leaving him with six young children. Maria's sister, Elizabeth Branwell, moved from her home in Cornwall to take over her late sister's responsibilities for the family. Until her death in 1842, she performed her role with diligence if not enthusiasm. She never really came to terms with moving from the

HAWORTH
THE HEART OF BRONTE COUNTRY

A village which has retained its quaint charms and is steeped in literary history

Old railway poster showing
Main Street, Haworth.

Top Withens.

warmth, colour and softness of her native Cornwall and its people to the hard bleak drabness of Haworth and its surroundings.

The tragedy continued with the deaths of Maria (May 1825) and Elizabeth (June 1825) following a spell at Cowan Bridge School, at eleven and ten years of age respectively.

The remaining four children grew to adulthood. The sisters took various posts as teachers and governesses and also spent time together at their home in Haworth, all intensively engaged in writing poetry, plays and stories and in creating their fictional worlds of Angria and Gondal. Likewise, Branwell wrote poetry, had a spell as a tutor and attempted to establish a career as a painter. Charlotte (twice) and Emily (once) spent several months in Brussels studying at the school of M. Heger. Here, Charlotte was conscious of being a Protestant in a Roman Catholic environment and also fell in love with M. Heger. When at home, significantly, they all walked extensively, spending much time on the adjacent moor.

The Parsonage, Haworth.

Portrait of the Brontë sisters, *c*.1834 (oil on canvas),
by Patrick Branwell Brontë.

Publication of their work was achieved only with difficulty.
Because they believed that novels by females were unlikely to be
accepted, the sisters sent manuscripts to several publishers under
assumed names: Acton (Anne), Currer (Charlotte) and Ellis (Emily)
Bell. Charlotte's first novel, *The Professor*, based on her Belgian
experiences, was rejected and was not published until after her death
in 1855. The breakthrough was the publication of Charlotte's *Jane
Eyre*, which was an instant success; then Emily's *Wuthering Heights*
and Anne's *Agnes Grey* in 1847, followed by Anne's *The Tenant of
Wildfell Hall* in the following year. In 1849, Charlotte's *Shirley* was

The wedding register at Haworth Parish Church.

published; her final novel, *Villette*, again based on her experiences in Brussels, appeared in print in 1852. During this period, confusion concerning the identity of the authors had remained, many believing that the books had been written by one person; in 1848 Charlotte and Anne travelled to London to prove their separate identities.

Meanwhile Branwell, having failed to turn his undoubted talents into any significant achievement, comforted himself with excessive alcohol and opium, hastening his death at the Parsonage in 1848. Even worse was to follow. Just two months later, Emily died; despite obvious and extreme symptoms of tuberculosis she had refused medical treatment until the day of her death. In May 1849, Anne, again with the symptoms of advanced tuberculosis, requested a last journey to Scarborough, a place she had visited during a spell as a governess to a family in the York area; she believed that the sea air might be beneficial. Within four days of her arrival she was dead. Her burial at Scarborough means that she is the only member of the family not to be interred in the vault in the churchyard at Haworth. After the burial, Charlotte returned home. From being one of four close-knit adult siblings, in a short space of time she had become the sole survivor, supporting her father; they were now the only two persons (apart from servants) occupying the Parsonage. She wrote to a servant, Martha Brown:

'I tried to be glad that I was coming home. I have always been glad before – except once – even then I was cheered. But this time joy was not to be the sensation. I felt that the house was all silent – the rooms were all empty. I remembered where the three were laid – in what narrow dark dwellings – never more to reappear on earth. So the sense of desolation and of bitterness took possession of me. The agony that was to be undergone, and was not to be avoided, came on. I underwent it, and passed a dreary evening and night, and a mournful morrow; today I am better.

'I do not know how life will pass, but I certainly do feel confidence in Him who has upheld me hitherto. Solitude may be cheered, and made endurable beyond what I can believe.' (Elizabeth Gaskell, *Life of Charlotte Brontë*, chapter 17)

After a delay due to her father's opposition and her own early indifference, Charlotte married Arthur Bell Nicholls, who had been her father's curate since 1844 (although he had departed temporarily when she rejected his first proposal). The couple were happy and Charlotte soon became pregnant, but her health was failing. Her recent friendships with the Kay-Shuttleworth family, Mrs Elizabeth Gaskell and Harriet Martineau could only be short term. Colds and chills intensified her malaise; she died on 31 March 1855.

THIS WAS THE SITE OF THE GATE LEADING TO THE CHURCH, USED BY THE BRONTE FAMILY, AND THROUGH WHICH THEY WERE CARRIED TO THEIR FINAL RESTING PLACE IN THE CHURCH.

Patrick lived in lonely old age until June 1861, when he became the last of the seven members of the Brontë family to be carried on that short journey to the churchyard through the gate at the bottom of the Parsonage garden.

Plaque in Haworth churchyard.

1. COWAN BRIDGE

The hamlets of Cowan Bridge, Overtown and Burrow, together with Tunstall Church, are linked by this circuit through the farmland adjacent to the River Leck. There is very little ascent and the walking is generally easy, with few stiles. A fair proportion is on roadsides, but the road used for much of the outward route is a very quiet lane and even the A683 through Burrow is not unduly busy. Crossing the fields above Churchfield House gives a good impression of the likely conditions underfoot endured by the Brontës and other children on their way to church, presumably wearing thin, inadequate shoes and clothing; superimpose winter conditions of cold, wind and wet and you will appreciate the severity of their weekly ordeal. The return route is an

Tunstall Church.

attractive ramble, largely close to the River Leck.
Cowan Bridge has visible remains of the long-defunct
Little North Western Railway, which connected the Settle
and Carlisle Railway at Clapham with the West Coast Main
Line south of Penrith. There is the site of a Roman fort
near Burrow.

The thirteenth-century Tunstall Church was rebuilt
early in the fifteenth century. The gallery used by the
pupils from the school was removed later in the nineteenth
century. The room over the porch remains but, after the
removal of the gallery, the only access is now by ladder.

DISTANCE	10km (6¼ miles)
ASCENT	35m (115ft)
START/PARKING	Car park at the Fraser Hall, behind the village shop at Cowan Bridge, grid reference 635765.
REFRESHMENTS	Highwayman Inn at Burrow; Cowan Bridge Tea Room.
MAP	Ordnance Survey Explorer OL2, Yorkshire Dales, Southern and Western areas, 1:25,000.

THE WALK

Ⓢ Walk back to the main road (A65); cross the road
and take a minor road opposite, signposted to Overtown.
Follow this road, which is nothing more than a country
lane, through a generally flat rural area for approximately
3.2km, passing Harren House and a large building
apparently converted into holiday accommodation.
The roadside walking is generally pleasant, with very
little traffic.

① Pass through Overtown hamlet, keeping left at a junction to pass Overtown Farm and Moy Park. The road rises at a gentle gradient. Several miles to the left the high ground of Goodber Common is in view. Pass the end of the Parkside Farm access drive, where the road skirts a narrow belt of woodland on the right.

② 200m after the farm access, as the road bends to the right, turn left to take the right-hand of two tracks (not the track leading to Cowdber Farm). Initially the track is a broad, rough stony roadway, soon passing a large agricultural building, where the roadway ends. There are gates as the route continues the same line; keep close to a fence on the right to pass a stone barn. Ingleborough is in view to the left. The barely visible path goes over grass to another gate. Go over a stile beside a gate with a battered waymark. Go through yet another gate and over more grass, with Churchfield House and its large outbuildings, apparently converted to holiday accommodation, in view ahead. Descend to a kissing gate and follow a tarmac roadway through the complex.

The remaining portion of the former Cowan Bridge School.

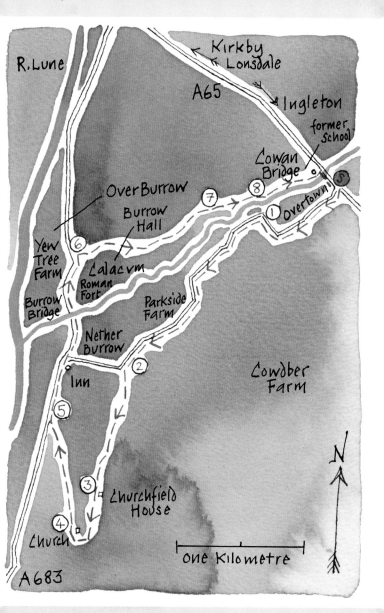

③ Continue along the access drive. Join a public road, turning right to reach Tunstall Church in 100m. Surrounded by a trim churchyard, with attractive trees, the church is beautifully kept and claims to be always open to visitors.

④ Leave the churchyard through a little gate behind the church and cross a large cultivated field (at some times of year a diversion around the edge of the field might be preferred). The right of way heads almost due north, to a little gate at the far end. Cross an overgrown area (a former lane?) to another little gate, almost opposite, with a bridleway waymark. Cross a huge meadow, bearing a little to the left, to reach a gate giving access to the main road, the A683.

⑤ Turn right to walk by the roadside, to the hamlet of Nether Burrow. Pass the Highwayman Inn, cross the River Leck and continue past the gates of Burrow Hall.

⑥ After passing Yew Tree Farm, turn right along a farm roadway (not that leading to Gamekeeper's Cottage). Go through the complex of farm buildings, through a gate and along an unsurfaced lane, passing an isolated building. Aim for a waymarked ladder stile over a wall ahead; then stay fairly close to the boundary on the left of a rising meadow. Go through a gate at the top, continuing close to the fence on the left, with great views to the Pennine Hills ahead.

⑦ At the bottom do not cross the obvious bridge; instead go through a gate and bear right to cross the stream a few metres further ahead. Continue, passing more gates at the side of stock pens. Cross a meadow, bearing right, to a gate/ladder stile. Join a surfaced access road and turn left along the side of the River Leck, which is very attractive and carpeted with bluebells in May.

⑧ As the road bends sharply to the left, fork right, along a narrow but clearly defined footpath, staying close to the river as far as the original Cowan Bridge, where there is a weir and pool. Go through a kissing gate and bear left to go up to the road, and turn right there, over the bridge, to return to the car park.

Squeezer stile, Tunstall Church.

This walk has very specific Brontë associations, both with their lives and with Charlotte's novel *Jane Eyre*, which is so detailed as to leave no doubt whatsoever concerning either places or people. Much of the route is literally in the footsteps of the often sad little Brontë girls and their school companions.

The school at Cowan Bridge (Lowood in the novel) was opened on 10 January 1824 by William Carus Wilson (Brocklehurst). Wilson was a wealthy clergyman who wanted to help comparatively impoverished clergy by educating their daughters in accordance with the strict Christian principles of the time. He charged very modest fees and his aims were entirely charitable. He bought a row of sixteenth-century cottages a short distance from the little River Leck, adding wings at right angles to each end of the terrace. At the front of the school was a substantial garden area, used by the girls for recreational purposes, including the cultivation of individual plots. The school soon had about forty-five pupils, with appropriate teaching and domestic staff. The surrounding area was countryside, entirely pleasant in summer, as Jane Eyre describes:

> I discovered, too, that a great pleasure, an enjoyment which the horizon only bounded, lay all outside the high and spike-guarded walls of our garden: this pleasure consisted in prospect of noble summits girdling a great hill-hollow rich in verdure and shadow: in a bright beck, full of dark stones and sparkling eddies. (*Jane Eyre*, chapter 9)

However, in winter the cold, the wind, the rain and an apparently inherently damp site all contributed to an unhealthy environment.

> The garden was a wide enclosure, surrounded with walls so high as to exclude every glimpse of prospect; a covered veranda ran down one side, and broad walks bordered a middle space divided into scores of little beds: these beds were assigned as gardens for the pupils to cultivate, and each bed had an owner. When full of flowers they would

doubtless look pretty; but now, at the latter end of January, all was wintry blight and brown decay. I shuddered as I stood and looked around me. It was an inclement day for outdoor exercise; not positively rainy, but darkened by a drizzly yellow fog; all under foot was still soaking wet with the floods of yesterday. The stronger among the girls ran about and engaged in active games, but sundry pale and thin ones herded together for shelter and warmth in the veranda; and amongst these, as the dense mist penetrated to their shivering frames, I heard frequently the sound of a hollow cough. (*Jane Eyre*, chapter 5)

Plaque on the gable wall of the former Cowan Bridge School.

The unhealthy environment was much exacerbated by the food at the school, described at great length by Mrs Elizabeth Gaskell in her *Life of Charlotte Brontë* (chapter 4). As always, Wilson believed that he was acting in the interests of his pupils. He purchased food of good quality; the problem was the cook, described by Mrs Gaskell as 'careless, dirty and wasteful'. It is clear that much of what was served to the unfortunate girls was inedible and that prolonged hunger made a significant contribution to the difficulties and tragedies that beset the school. When confronted about the inedible food, Wilson's fictional counterpart Brocklehurst used the occasion to deliver a mini sermon, concluding:

'Oh madam, when you put bread and cheese, instead of burnt porridge, into these children's mouths, you may indeed feed their vile bodies, but you little think how you starve their immortal souls.' (*Jane Eyre*, chapter 7)

A further contribution to the rigours of the lives of the girls was the walk each Sunday to and from the church at Tunstall (Brocklebridge Church, Lowton, in *Jane Eyre*), where Wilson was the vicar. At the cold, inhospitable church the often shivering girls had to stay for morning and afternoon services, separated by a meagre cold lunch, reputedly eaten in the small chamber over the church's entrance porch:

Sundays were dreary days in that winter season. We had to walk two miles to Brocklebridge Church . . . We set out cold, we arrived at church colder; during the morning service we became almost paralyzed. It was too far to return to dinner, and an allowance of cold meat and bread, in the same penurious proportion observed in our ordinary meals, was served round between the services.

At the close of the afternoon service we returned by an exposed and hilly road, where the bitter winter wind, blowing over a range of snowy summits to the north, almost flayed the skin from our faces. (*Jane Eyre*, chapter 7)

Into this environment came the two eldest Brontë sisters, Maria and Elizabeth, in July 1824. Already weakened by whooping cough, chickenpox and measles the previous winter, neither child was fit to withstand the hard life at Cowan Bridge School. Maria (Helen Burns in *Jane Eyre*), a bright child with wonderful stoicism in adversity, also suffered from harsh treatment by an unsympathetic member of staff. A few weeks later the sisters were joined at the school by Charlotte and then Emily.

Old chest, Tunstall Church.

The general malaise was apparently greatly exacerbated in spring 1825, when fever broke out at the school; Wilson sought the best possible medical advice. In a very poor state of health Maria and Elizabeth returned home to Haworth the same spring. Within a few days Maria died, followed by Elizabeth a few weeks later. In both cases the symptoms were of consumption (tuberculosis). Surprisingly Charlotte and Emily returned to Cowan Bridge, finally leaving the school before the next winter.

The alleged fever outbreak has since been disputed by many who believe that Charlotte was rather hard on Wilson and his school. Mrs Gaskell also clearly felt some sympathy for Wilson. Very much a product of his time and his background, even when later proved to have been manifestly wrong he believed that he was acting in the interests of his pupils.

> But Mr. Wilson seems to have had the unlucky gift of irritating those to whom he meant kindly, and for whom he was making perpetual sacrifices of time and money, by never showing any respect for their independence of opinion and action. He had, too, so little knowledge of human nature.
> (Mrs Elizabeth Gaskell, *Life of Charlotte Brontë*, chapter 4)

The school closed in 1833. The wings added by Wilson were destroyed by fire later in the nineteenth century but the cottages remain, in private occupation, with an appropriate plaque on the roadside gable.

2. APPERLEY BRIDGE AND AIREDALE

Although close to extensive urban areas, the length of Airedale to the east of Apperley Bridge is remarkably rural, a peaceful backwater. The canal, railway and well-used footpaths all stay close to the valley bottom, combining to provide an attractive circuit. No hills to climb, very few stiles and uniformly good tracks all contribute to an easy and enjoyable walk. The return is along the towpath of the Leeds and Liverpool Canal.

DISTANCE	7.75km (4¾ miles)
ASCENT	Negligible
START/PARKING	Roadside parking on a minor link road to the west of the main road from Bradford to Yeadon (A658), approximately 100m north of the river crossing, grid reference 195380.
REFRESHMENTS	Stansfield Arms Inn, close to start/finish; Bridge Café, close to the bridge; a signposted inn close to Owl Bridge.
MAP	Ordnance Survey Explorer 288, Bradford and Huddersfield, 1:25,000.

THE WALK

Ⓢ Go to the main road, crossing over to the entrance to Woodhouse Grove School. Go ahead along a waymarked footpath beside the school's entrance drive. The footpath bears right, and then left, to a signpost. Continue along

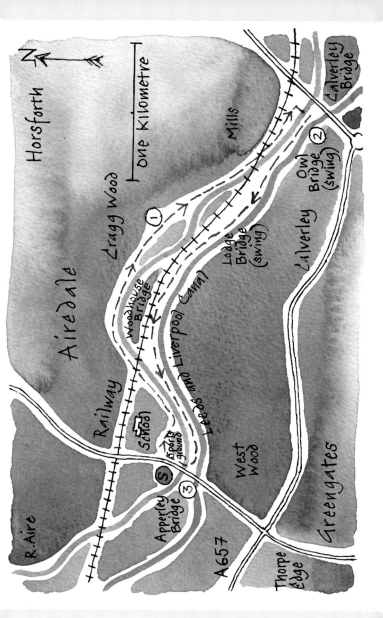

Woodhouse Grove School, Apperley Bridge.

the excellent path, over a stone stile, past another signpost and under a railway bridge. For some distance the path stays close to the River Aire, and is quite unmistakable, before bearing a little to the left, along the bottom edge of a wooded hillside.

① Pass a house, and go up to the left before bearing right to continue. At a fork go right, on a more minor path, winding through the trees, close to the river. Cross a bridge over a stream; to the left are modern factories. Go under the railway again at a double bridge, cross a meadow and turn right, up steps, at the end. Turn right to cross a cobble-surfaced bridge over the River Aire, with great views upstream and downstream. After the bridge go up a flight of steps ahead, turn right along a roadway for a few metres and join the towpath of the Leeds and Liverpool Canal.

②At a swing bridge (Owl Bridge), where there is a sign for an inn and a 'public footpath, Apperley Bridge' signpost, turn right to follow the towpath all the way back to Apperley Bridge. The generous towpath accommodates both cyclists and walkers and there are a few wayside seats. The scenery is gently pastoral; after you pass, without crossing, a swing bridge, one section is alongside woodland. Pass a milepost – 'Liverpool 119 miles, Leeds 8½ miles'. The towpath goes above a farm and under an iron bridge before reaching the main road.

③Go up steps to the right to join the road, turn right and follow the wide roadside footpath across the river bridge to return to the parking place.

Leeds and Liverpool Canal, near Apperley Bridge.

In June 1812, Maria Branwell, whose home was in Penzance, was staying with her aunt and uncle, the Fennells, at Woodhouse Grove School, Apperley Bridge. Patrick Brontë visited the school with a former Wellington colleague, William Morgan, now a curate at Bradford Parish Church, as an examiner in the classics. Morgan was engaged to the Fennells' daughter Jane.

Railway bridge over the River Aire, near Apperley Bridge.

After a brief courtship, Maria and Patrick were married at Guiseley Parish Church, a short distance to the north of Apperley Bridge, on 29 December 1812 in a double ceremony with William Morgan and Jane Fennell. Each bridegroom officiated at the other's wedding.

3. BRONTË WAY: OAKWELL HALL TO HARTSHEAD

Oakwell Hall.

The Brontë Way is a linear footpath approximately 67.5km (42 miles) in length, linking sites with Brontë associations. The sites are either places where they lived or were employed or which provided settings for their novels. At the eastern end of the Way is Oakwell Hall, near Birstall. At the western end is Gawthorpe Hall, near Burnley. Between the two, the Way encompasses a wide variety of landscapes, ranging from the wild moors above Haworth to the industrial areas to the south and south-west of Bradford.

This walk is at the east end of the Way. It twists and turns through former industrial areas such as Gomersal and Liversedge, in a landscape that is a mixture of urban and rural, as is typical of this part of West Yorkshire. There are plenty of stiles, no difficult ascents, generally good tracks and a fair distance on roadside pavement.

Oakwell Hall, open to the public, is now the focal point of an attractive country park, managed by Kirklees Council. As early as the fourteenth century coal was dug from outcropping seams at Oakwell. Spasmodic mining of the shallower deposits through the centuries culminated in the sinking of deep shafts early in the twentieth century. From 1916 until its closure in 1973 Gomersal was a working coal mine; part of the surface area is now occupied by the Oakwell Hall car park.

The Red House is another very attractive old house, managed by Kirklees Council as a visitor attraction.

To visit Birstall Church, a short diversion close to the start of the walk is required.

As this is not a circular walk, either return by bus – 229 to Heckmondwike, and then 209 to Oakwell Country Park (infrequent) – or by retracing the route.

DISTANCE	8km (5 miles)
ASCENT	118m (387ft)
START/PARKING	Car park at Oakwell Hall, grid reference 218271.
REFRESHMENTS	Café at Oakwell Hall; inns along the way (some not open at lunchtime).
MAP	Ordnance Survey Explorer 288, Bradford and Huddersfield, 1:25,000..

THE WALK

Ⓢ Walk back to the main vehicular gateway of the car park. Turn left for a few metres, and then right at a 'public bridleway' sign. A well-used track descends gently in a straight line, initially between horse paddocks.

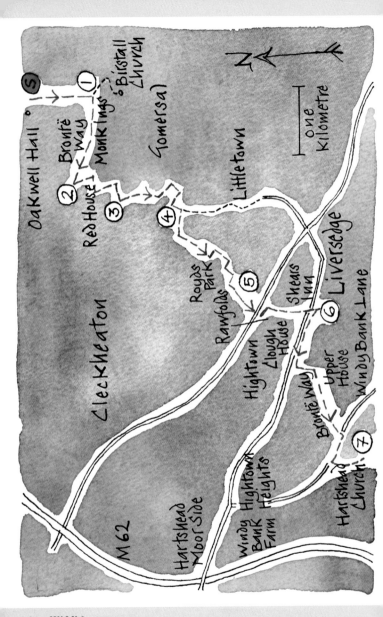

Oakwell Hall

S

① 'Bistall Church

Brontë Way

Monkings

(Gomersal)

② ③ Red House

Littletown

④

Cleckheaton

Royds Park

Ranfolds

⑤ Shears Inn

⑥ Liversedge

Windy Bank Lane

Hightown

Clough House

Upper House

Brontë Way

⑦

Hartshead Church

M62

Hartshead Moor Side

Windy Bank Farm

Hightown Heights

one Kilometre

① Join the A652 main road. Go straight across to Monk Ings, a cul-de-sac housing estate. (To visit Birstall Church, turn left to walk along the pavement of the A652 as far as the next right turn. The church is a short distance along this road. Return to Monk Ings to resume the walk.) Continue up Monk Ings for approximately 130m. Fork left along an unsurfaced roadway with a 'public footpath' signpost. At the top is a field gate, with stile. Go through to follow the same line, across three gently rising fields. Towards the top of the third field bear right to a waymark on a post and a clear track between walls. Pass school playing fields on the left to reach a small housing estate. Bear left to reach another main road, the A651.

② Turn left along the roadside pavement, cross the road opposite Gomersal Public Hall and turn left to reach Red House car park in a few metres. The Red House, an important Brontë feature, is to the left of the car park. To continue the walk go across the grass at the rear of the car park, pass through an opening in a wall and turn left along a hard-surfaced path with a housing estate to the right.

Red House, Gomersal.

A typical nineteenth–century West Yorkshire textile mill.

Birstall Parish Church.

③ At the main road turn right, cross the road and turn left at Shirley Road, by the side of St Mary's Church. Follow Shirley Road to its far end, where it joins Upper Lane. Cross over, go through a stile and keep to the edge of a large recreation area, descending. Join Lower Lane and turn right.

④ Immediately after the road bends to the right, turn left to take a path adjacent to the driveway of a private house. Keep a stone wall on the right, and at a waymarked junction keep right. Go over a stile and continue along a field path. Go straight ahead, through a gate, along a track with a hedge on the right. At the end of the track bear to the left to cross a field on a reasonably clear path with extensive views over the Spen Valley. Go over a stile and turn left along an old, part-sunken track, which soon bears to the right, descending. At a 'Private Road' sign, turn left at a waymarked stile, angle down to the right, go over a stile at the bottom and join a surfaced cycleway. Turn right and then immediately left, through the end of Royds Park, to join the main road.

(5) Cross the road, turn right and then, after 40m, turn left at Primrose Lane, which has a 'public bridleway' sign. After 50m the lane becomes an unsurfaced track. To the right is the site of the long-demolished Rawfolds Mill. The track rises steadily up the side of the valley, passing under a disused railway line before reaching Halifax Road at the top. The Shears Inn is a few metres to the left of the route.

(6) Turn right to walk along the roadside footpath for 0.8km. Opposite Clough Lane is Clough House, another Brontë feature. Turn left to go along Clough Lane as far as the bridge across Clough Beck (the original bridge is to the right). Immediately after the bridge turn sharp right at a 'public footpath' sign, over a stile, and follow a faint path rising close to a stone wall on the left. Go through a gate at the top, pass through the buildings of Upper House Farm and continue along the farm access road (Upper House Lane). At the end of the access road go straight ahead along a public road to reach a main road (Thorn Bush Farm is across the fields to the right). Turn right, and then immediately left, to visit St Peter's Church, Hartshead.

(7) Return to Oakwell Hall. There are bus stops on the main road, quite close to the church.

The route of this walk, among several of the lesser former industrial settlements of West Yorkshire, is through the heart of what has become known as Shirley Country. Charlotte Brontë's novel *Shirley* was published in 1849, but was set in 1812, a year of vigorous activity by the Luddites, militant groupings of workers in the woollen industry whose hand-crafted operations (and livelihoods) were threatened by the introduction of new machinery in ever larger factories. In particular, the novel replicates a real-life attack by the Luddites, planned at the Shears Inn, Hightown, on Rawfolds Mill, which became Charlotte's Hollows Mill. Heroines Shirley and Caroline watch in terror from near by.

The characters in the novel are based on real-life people: heroine Caroline Helstone is modelled on Charlotte's sister Anne and also on a schoolfriend, Ellen Nussey, while Shirley contains a good deal of Charlotte herself. The real-life forthright Revd Hammond Roberson, a friend of Patrick Brontë, became the Revd Mathewson Helstone, a strong opponent of the Luddites.

On their way to Rawfolds Mill, the bands of Luddites would have passed close by Lousey Thorn Farm (now Thorn

St Peter's Church, Hartshead.

Bush Farm), where Patrick Brontë lodged while he was curate at Hartshead in 1812. Despite his friendship with Hammond Roberson, who aided the owner in his successful defence of the besieged mill, it is hard to imagine that Patrick, a young man from a poor Irish background, would not have felt sympathy with these unfortunate workers. Subsequently Patrick carried a small gun for personal protection.

Rawfolds is long demolished, as are most of the similar mills in the area, largely replaced by unattractive utilitarian commercial structures.

Charlotte frequently visited the Elizabethan manor house Oakwell Hall, and it becomes Fieldhead in *Shirley*.

> If Fieldhead had few other merits as a building, it might
> at least be termed picturesque: its irregular architecture,
> and the grey and mossy colouring communicated by time
> gave it a just claim to this epithet. (*Shirley*, chapter 11)

The Red House at nearby Gomersal dates from 1660 but has been restored to the atmosphere of the 1830s and open to the public. It was the home of Mary Taylor, a close friend of Charlotte whom she met when she went to Miss Wooler's school at Roe Head in 1831–2 – comparatively happy years. Charlotte often stayed at the Red House. In *Shirley* the house became Briarmains and Mary's family the Yorkes. Birstall Parish Church became Briarfield in *Shirley*.

St Peter's Church, Hartshead, is where Patrick Brontë was curate from 1811 to 1815. Clough House, Hightown, is where he set up house with his wife Maria in January 1813, after their marriage in 1812, and where their first two children, Maria (January 1814) and Elizabeth (February 1815) were born. A month after Elizabeth's birth Patrick changed livings and the family moved to Thornton.

4. SHIBDEN HALL

A very attractive house dating from 1420, Shibden Hall stands in an extensive park on the fringes of Halifax. The hall is owned and managed as a visitor attraction by Calderdale District Council. Attractions include a boating lake, children's play area, narrow gauge railway and café.

This circuit rises high on the side of the valley of the Shibden Brook, running largely through the farmland of Southowram, an area of former mining and quarrying activity. Tracks are good throughout; there is a fair amount of ascent, mainly in the initial rise from Shibden Park.

DISTANCE	6.5km (4 miles)
ASCENT	180m (607ft)
START/PARKING	Car parks serving Shibden Hall: upper car park entered direct from the public road, lower car park by the side of the hall, accessed by an internal roadway from the upper car park, grid reference (lower) 106258. Note that the road access to Shibden Hall and also separate access to the associated parkland and visitor centre are very specific. From the Halifax direction (to the hall), fork left from the A58 (east) a short distance after a major roundabout. This minor road crosses back over the A58 on a bridge before reaching the upper car park.
REFRESHMENTS	Café at Shibden Hall.
MAP	Ordnance Survey Explorer 288, Bradford and Huddersfield, 1:25,000.

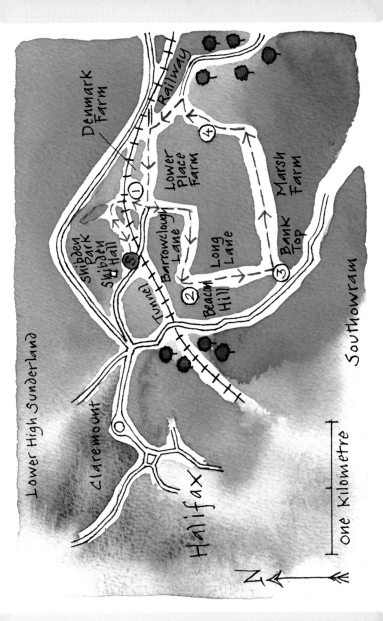

Shibden Hall.

THE WALK

Ⓢ From the car park beside the hall go to a nearby signpost. Turn sharp right to follow a park roadway passing below the buildings of the hall. Pass a lily pond, with information boards, before turning left at an adjacent junction to follow a broad track descending through woodland, heading for the children's playground. At a junction with a surfaced roadway go right to pass through the play area. After the play area, by the end of the adjacent lake turn right, up a cobbled way, to leave the park, pass under a railway line and continue up along an old paved track as far as a public road.

① Cross the road, turn left for a few metres and then turn right into Shibden Hall Croft. Turn right after 20m and then left after 40m to follow a good broad track between walls, rising steadily. There are soon long views over the valley of Shibden Brook, towards

Hipperholme. At a junction with the unsurfaced Barrowclough Lane, turn right to follow the lane, still rising. The next junction has various waymarks; carry on along the lane, again with fine long views.

② At a junction beside a high stone wall turn sharp left. This is Long Lane. (The site of the demolished High Sunderland Hall is about 1.6km north of this point.) Beacon Hill and Beacon House are to the right. Go gently downhill to reach part of Bank Top, with a surfaced road. Go straight ahead for less than 200m to join another road. (Law Hill lies about 0.4km ahead; you can reach it as a diversion from this walk by turning right, and then left, to join a more important road. Turn left for a short distance.)

③ Turn left to walk by the roadside for approximately 400m. Pass the end of Marsh Delves Lane and then fork right

to take a broad track to Marsh Farm. Ignore a waymarked path on the right, continuing past the buildings to follow a broad straight track and descending gently through upland agriculture, rough pasture and stone walls, many of them broken. This was also an area of mining and quarrying in previous centuries. On reaching a storage compound turn left to take a track descending more steeply.

④ At the bottom join a minor roadway, turning right, downhill. Pass hairpin bends, staying with the roadway at a junction. Pass a row of cottages; a few metres further on turn left to take a minor path, signposted 'public footpath to Shibden Hall Road'. The path is always clear on the ground, soon joining the road, up a few steps. Turn left to walk along the roadside pavement for about 0.8km, passing Denmark Farm. Turn right at point 1 of the outward route to return to Shibden Hall.

Dark Lane, on the Magma Via, Calderdale.

The garden at Shibden Hall.

Shibden Hall is just one of the houses that are believed to have influenced Emily Brontë in her description of Thrushcross Grange in *Wuthering Heights*. Thrushcross Grange was the home of the Linton family in that novel, set on the moor above Haworth, just a few miles from Wuthering Heights itself, on the site of the present Ponden Hall (see walk 11), but was an altogether less exposed, more comfortable residence than Wuthering Heights.

In 1837 Emily Brontë taught for some months at Law Hill School, situated high on the side of the valley of the Shibden Brook in the Southowram area. The most home-loving of the sisters, dedicated to Haworth and its moor, Emily was very unhappy in what seems to have been an over-demanding employment. During this comparatively short period she became familiar with the area, its landscape and, as Law Hill was also a farm, with the farming activities that are mentioned in *Wuthering Heights*. Not surprisingly, with its high, windswept situation, Law Hill was regarded by many as the model for

Wuthering Heights. However, not far away and on the same side of the valley was High Sunderland Hall, unfortunately demolished in 1950. Wuthering Heights as described by Lockwood in chapter 1 of the novel has great similarity with the former High Sunderland Hall, which gives it probably the best claim of the various contenders. The strong probability is that no single building or place was copied in total, but that Emily (as did her sisters) used her creative imagination, drawing on her familiarity with a number of premises and locations to form her images of Wuthering Heights and Thrushcross Grange.

Some decorative stonework from the former High Sunderland Hall is preserved at Shibden Hall.

Another intriguing local name is Black Boy House, close to the site of High Sunderland Hall. This is a very unusual name for a property in a traditional West Yorkshire rural situation. Emily described her pivotal character Heathcliffe as 'a dark skinned gypsy' (*Wuthering Heights*, chapter 1) and later refers to him as a 'lascar' (of a mixed race of south-east Asians, traditionally seamen). Could she have been influenced by this curious place name?

Garden features at Shibden Hall.

5. LUDDENDEN FOOT AND MYTHOLMROYD

Bridge over the Rochdale Canal.

Considering that the valley of the River Calder was very much a cradle of the feverish activity of the Industrial Revolution and was (and is) also a vital linking route between the industrial areas of Lancashire and Yorkshire by road, rail and canal, this walk is surprisingly rural for much of its length. The outward route uses the excellent towpath of the Rochdale Canal, and the return is along a cycleway/footpath created in recent years, partially wooded and never very far from the still operational railway line.

After several earlier proposals and surveys of possible routes, construction of the Rochdale Canal commenced in 1794; it was completed and opened in 1804, the first of the three routes which link Lancashire and Yorkshire across the Pennines. Although only 53km (33 miles) in length, it was an ambitious undertaking, for it crosses difficult terrain, aided by no fewer than ninety-two locks. At the Manchester end it linked with the Bridgewater Canal, at Sowerby Bridge with the Calder and Hebble Navigation.

After the construction of the Manchester and Leeds Railway in the 1840s, canal profitability declined, with eventual takeover by the railway company. The last commercial boat passed through in 1937; closure followed in 1952. A colossal restoration project culminated in full navigational reopening in July 2002.

Neither Luddenden Foot nor Mytholmroyd has features of great interest but the latter has a good selection of shops and inns.

DISTANCE	6.5km (4 miles)
ASCENT	25m (82ft)
START/PARKING	Small car park at Station Road, Luddenden Foot, grid reference 038250.
REFRESHMENTS	Inns and cafés at Luddenden Foot and Mytholmroyd.
MAP	Ordnance Survey Explorer OL21, South Pennines, 1:25,000.

THE WALK

Ⓢ The car park adjoins the canal towpath. Turn left to walk along the towpath, a very pleasant route, under bridges and passing two locks, no. 5 and no. 6 (Upper Brearley). There are waterfowl and, apart from some traffic noise from the nearby road, a gentle rural charm prevails. As the towpath forks keep right, going up to cross a minor road. Reach the commercial fringe of Mytholmroyd, continuing almost to the point where the canal passes under the main road.

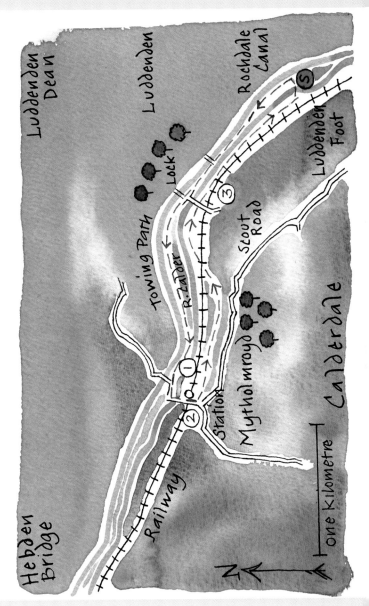

Luddenden Dean

Luddenden

Luddenden Foot

Rochdale Canal

Towing Path

Lock

R. Calder

Scout Road

Mytholmroyd

Calderdale

Hebden Bridge

Railway

Station

one kilometre

N

① Approximately 70m short of the main road bear left to leave the towpath. Head for the main road, cross over and turn left to walk along the roadside pavement for approximately 250m, passing the church. At pedestrian crossing lights turn left. Cross the river on a footbridge, after which you soon pass under the railway line.

② Turn left up the station approach ramp. There are cycleway signs to 'Luddenden Foot and Sowerby Bridge' and a waymark. From the station approach go ahead along an attractive permissive woodland path, staying close to the railway. The track forks; the paths stay close together and either is satisfactory. After the paths rejoin, bear left to cross the railway on a footbridge before reaching a surfaced lane and passing dwellings, including an apparent former chapel. The lane returns towards the railway line.

Sowerby Bridge canal basin: Calder and Hebble Navigation, West Yorkshire.

3 Immediately before the railway bridge, leave the lane to take a cycleway path on the left; this soon rises up a ramp to continue by the side of the railway to Luddenden Foot, reached through a depot for old buses. The cycleway is marked on the ground through the depot. Turn right for a few metres along Old Station Road, and then left down Station Road to return to the car park.

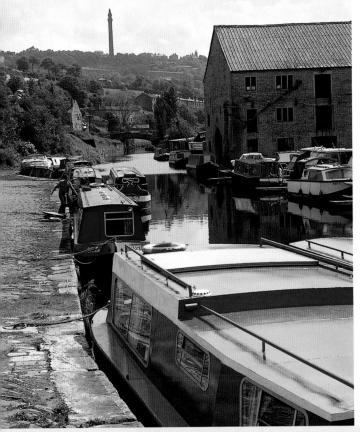

His brief career in the service of the Manchester and Leeds Railway is just one of the unsuccessful episodes in the sad life of the undoubtedly talented Patrick Branwell Brontë. When the railway came to Sowerby Bridge and the station was opened in October 1840, Branwell was appointed to the post of Assistant Clerk in Charge. Later, he was promoted to the post of Clerk in Charge at the next station along the line, Luddenden Foot. Although these were not very senior posts, his service must have been sufficiently regarded by the company to justify the promotion and he

must have kept the temptations posed by the nearby inns sufficiently under control.

However, in 1842 Branwell was dismissed for being £11 (a considerable sum then) short in his accounts. There was no suggestion of dishonesty. It is hard to imagine a man of Branwell's background and personality being dedicated to a humdrum working life as a railway clerk; carelessness is generally accepted as the reason for the discrepancy.

While working at Luddenden Branwell had his first poem published in the *Halifax Guardian*. This was followed by twelve further poems; as Charlotte had said, 'the idea of being authors was as natural to the Brontës as walking'.

Sowerby Bridge station is still in use for passenger services between Leeds and Manchester. Luddenden Foot station was closed on 10 September 1962, the site now being occupied by a transport depot and other modern commercial premises. Station Road and Old Station Road remain as evidence of its existence.

Above: Self-portrait in profile (pencil on paper) by Patrick Branwell Brontë.
Left: An historic railway booking office on the Keighley and Worth Valley Railway.

6. THORNTON AND THE OLD BELL CHAPEL

The area to the south of Thornton is surprisingly attractive, with little valleys, farming land and hamlets such as West Scholes separating the built-up areas of Thornton and Queensbury. Not surprisingly, local industrialists very much wanted a railway connection between Bradford, Keighley and Halifax, also serving minor centres such as Queensbury. However, the hilly nature of the terrain posed severe difficulties. The Great Northern Railway Company opened a line in 1878 but Queensbury, in particular, had a problem. The station was about 1.6km (1 mile) from the town, along an unsurfaced and unlit footpath, with a height difference of 122km (400 feet). In 1890 a new station was opened, still rather distant, but of a triangular shape, with three platforms and a signal box at each corner. Because of its many difficulties the line was known as the 'Alpine Route'; Queensbury Tunnel was, at the time of construction, the longest on the Great Northern system. The still impressive Thornton Viaduct carried the line over Pinch Beck.

Since the closure of the line in 1956 the site of the former station – the 'Queensbury Triangle' – has become an important wildlife habitat.

In this walk there are three ascents, including the section rising to the Old Bell Chapel at Thornton, which is part of the Brontë Way; none is seriously steep. The footpaths are not difficult to follow but there are several stiles.

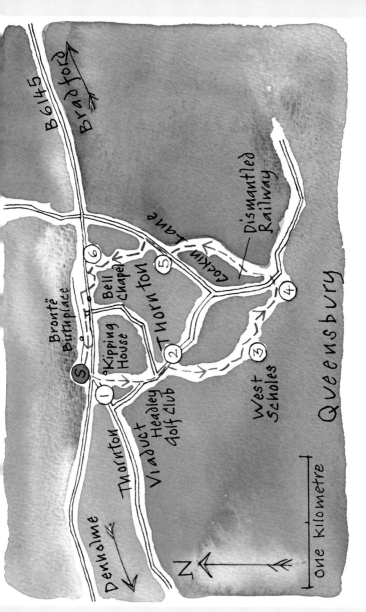

DISTANCE	6km (3¾ miles)
ASCENT	203m (666ft)
START/PARKING	Small car park off West Lane, Thornton, entered by the side of the Black Horse Inn, grid reference 099327. If full, there is plenty of roadside parking space close by.
REFRESHMENTS	Inns and café at Thornton, close to car park.
MAP	Ordnance Survey Explorer 288, Bradford and Huddersfield, 1:25000.

THE WALK

Ⓢ Walk down through the small roadside garden, pass an information board, cross the main road and continue along Lower Kipping Lane, with Kipping Barn on the left. Kipping House is the next house on the left. The great Thornton Viaduct is in view ahead.

① At a 'public footpath' sign on a lamp post turn left, through a gate, between houses, to follow a paved track descending the side of a shallow valley. Cross the stream on a footbridge and ascend the far side of the valley, part of a golf course. Go up steps at the top, soon reaching the former railway line. Bear left along a track just above the line, to reach a road. Turn right to cross a bridge.

② Turn left at once along a footpath signposted to West Scholes. Go through a squeezer stile and keep to the left edge of a field, descending to another stile. With a former railway bridge on the left, bear right for 20m;

then go through a waymarked gate on the left. The faint path angles to the right, descending across the hillside, heading for a stile and a tiny bridge over a stream. Go through a gate and up through a small wood. Go over a stile at the top, continuing with a wall on the left to reach a short lane and West Scholes hamlet.

③ Turn left at a rough surfaced road with signpost. After 100m turn right at a signpost 'public footpath, Marley Lane'. Descend a track between walls, soon reaching a public road. Turn left and then right at a junction after 100m for a steady descent to the former railway line. The settlements in view across the valley are Clayton, ahead, and Queensbury to the right. Pass a 'Welcome to Clayton' sign.

Ruin of the Old Bell Chapel, Thornton.

④ At the bottom is a former railway bridge, carrying what was part of the Queensbury Triangle (a path to the right leads up to the former track bed, now hard surfaced, but, alas, there is nothing to be seen of the three platforms, the three signal boxes or any other railway structures). Continue the circuit by forking left, under the railway bridge, along a concrete roadway leading to Hole Bottom Farm. There is a 'public footpath' sign. After 40m turn left to take a waymarked path passing above the farm and heading along the valley side. There are squeezer stiles as the path stays level, keeping generally close to a wall on the right. Go over a stile beside a gate to pass straight through a farmstead (Sunwood Barn), leaving by the access road.

⑤ Join the public road (Cockin Lane). Turn right; Thornton Church is in view to the left. Pass a road junction and in a further 30m turn left to follow the signposted Brontë Way along Corn Mill Lane. Descend to pass the site of the former corn mill before going through a gate, and then a stile, to walk up diagonally across a huge sloping meadow on a barely visible path, aiming to the right of the church. Go through a kissing gate at the top, and bear left, then right, to reach the main Bradford road. Thornton Hall is on the left.

⑥ Turn left by the roadside to reach the Old Bell Chapel on the left. Cross the road; immediately past the church turn right along a signposted footpath at the side of the church. Turn left at the far end of the path to walk by the roadside. The road becomes Market Street. The Brontës' birthplace is no. 74, which has a suitable plaque. Continue along Market Street; as it bears left back towards the main road, go ahead by the side of the Black Horse Inn into the car park.

Thornton viaduct.

Cupola of the Old Bell Chapel, Thornton.

This walk includes the 'birthplace' at 74 Market Street, Thornton (described in walk 7), and the Old Bell Chapel, also at Thornton.

The Old Bell Chapel, originally of 1612, is now a sparse ruin, occupying a site on the south of the main road, almost opposite the present parish church of St James.

Patrick Brontë was the incumbent (as perpetual curate) at Thornton from 1815 to 1820. He was responsible for the rebuilding of the Old Bell Chapel. The plain, rectangular structure was embellished by the addition of an octagonal cupola. Inside, the chapel had box pews and a three-decker pulpit. The font, where no fewer than five of the Brontë children were baptized, was moved across the road to the new church when it was constructed later in the nineteenth century. The ruins are now scant; most notable is the octagonal bell tower. The site has a useful illustrated information board.

Kipping House, on Kipping Lane, was the home of the Firth family, good friends of the Brontës. The diaries of Elizabeth Firth have survived, providing a record of some activities of the Brontë family. Mr Firth was the godfather of Elizabeth Brontë; Elizabeth Firth and Aunt Branwell were her godmothers. After the move to Haworth, the friendship between the Brontës and the Firths continued, visits being exchanged, particularly at times of illness.

Photograph of Patrick Brontë taken late in his life.

7. DENHOLME AND THORNTON

Thornton is a more attractive little town than might be expected from its proximity to the Bradford conurbation. Market Street is now a comparatively quiet residential thoroughfare, most traffic using the comparatively recent bypassing road, where many of the commercial premises are situated.

Doe Park Reservoir, close to Denholme village, is, like so many of the smaller reservoirs, an attractive sheet of water, used by a sailing club for recreational purposes.

The countryside between Denholme and Thornton is largely high-lying marginal agricultural land, dotted with small hamlets comprising unpretentious stone dwellings of indeterminate age, blending into the harsh landscape. The paths are very variable but not too difficult to follow and there are no steep ascents of any length. Inevitably, there are several stiles. In Thornton the route is along the pavement of moderately quiet roads. This walk includes part of the Brontë Way.

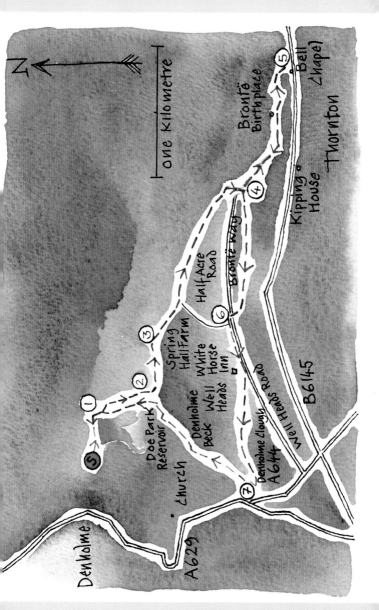

DENHOLME AND THORNTON 67

DISTANCE	9.5km (6 miles)
ASCENT	178m (584ft)
START/PARKING	Roadside spaces on a minor road in Denholme, a cul-de-sac leading to the foot of Doe Park Reservoir and the sailing club, grid reference 076341. From the main road through Denholme turn to the east a short distance to the north of the post office.
REFRESHMENTS	Inns at Thornton and Denholme; White Horse Inn, Well Heads Road, near Thornton.
MAP	Ordnance Survey Explorers OL21, South Pennines, and 288, Bradford and Huddersfield, 1:25,000.

THE WALK

Ⓢ Start down the road heading for the reservoir dam, passing the sailing club and a gate at the bottom. Cross the dam. Turn right, and then left through a signposted gate at the far end.

① Before passing above Kitchener House, turn left at a junction for a short, sharp rise up the valley side. As the path forks, keep right to follow a reasonable path at a higher level along the valley side. Across the valley, Denholme and its church are prominent. Eventually the path descends to reach a gap in a broken wall. Go through to reach a junction in a few metres. There is an old waymark on a tree and a redundant stile.

② Turn left to go up gently through woodland, with a stream on the right. Leave the woodland at a stile to continue across farmland. The path is now vague; keep close to a wall on the right, crossing two more fields before reaching a signposted stile giving access to a public road (Ten Yards Lane).

③ Turn right to walk by the roadside, passing Spring Hall Farm, to reach a road junction at a hamlet; a terrace of houses has the name Moscow. Cross the road, bearing left for a few metres and then right at a short roadway, with a terrace of houses on the right, to reach a squeezer stile and an old paved track. Pass a junction and a seat before descending a few steps to Wicken Lane, on the fringe of Thornton. Go left and then immediately turn right at a more major road, downhill. This is West Lane.

④ Fork to the left at a junction in approximately 100m (still West Lane) to continue the descent. Bear left at the bottom, along Market Street. The Brontës' birthplace is no. 74, marked by a plaque. Stay with Market Street and its continuation. When close to the parish church turn right at a footpath marked by a large 'Brontë Way' sign. Pass along the side of the church to reach the main road. Cross and turn left to the entrance to the Bell Chapel site.

⑤ Return by the same route to point 4. Cross the road to follow an unsurfaced roadway, with a footpath sign. This is the Brontë Way, a straight, clear path leading directly to a large cemetery. Pass straight through the cemetery. There are waymarks and gates as the Way continues. On approaching a public road turn right, uphill, along a farm track, to a stile giving access to the road, near a junction.

⑥ Turn left to walk by the roadside, passing the White Horse Inn. Approximately 200m after the inn turn right at a footpath leading directly into open fields. The path is very vague; keep close to a wall on the right. At the angle of the wall go half left across a field to join a concrete-surfaced farm roadway. Turn left to reach Morton End Farm. Immediately after passing the farm turn half right, aiming well to the left of Denholme Church, to follow a faint path descending across fields, separated by stiles. The path becomes clearer on the ground before it reaches the bottom of Denholme Clough.

Landscape near Thornton.

⑦ Turn sharp right. A generally good path descends gently along the bottom of the attractive valley, crossing the stream and passing under a former railway bridge before reaching the reservoir. Bear left and then turn right, across a little bridge, to follow an old path, with boardwalks. Go through two little gates to continue, rejoining the outward route at point 1. Retrace across the dam to return to the parking area.

This circuit includes the house occupied by Patrick Brontë and his growing family from 1815 to 1820, during his period as curate of Thornton, in the parish of Bradford: the 'birthplace', 74 Market Street. At this stage of his life Patrick was described (Elizabeth Gaskell, *Life of Charlotte Brontë*, chapter 3) as 'powerfully built, a very handsome fellow, full of Irish enthusiasm, with something of an Irishman's capability of falling in love'. Obviously the young Patrick was very different from the gloomy impression given by the well-known portrait and the accounts of his behaviour in later years.

At Thornton four Brontë children were born in rapid succession (the first two, Maria and Elizabeth, were born at Hartshead – see walk 3): Charlotte (1816), Patrick Branwell (1817), Emily (1818) and Anne (1820). All the births are recorded on the plaque at the front of the house. The projecting portion to the right of the door is a later addition.

The Brontës' birthplace, 74 Market Street, Thornton.

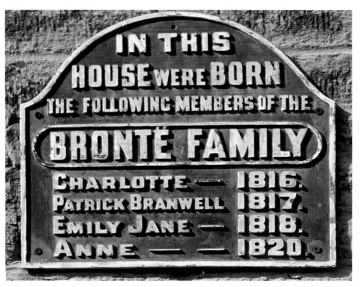

Plaque at the birthplace.

Despite (or perhaps because of) Maria's almost constant pregnancy, the impression is of a contented family life at Thornton, free of the tragedy that was soon to strike the Brontës. Among a circle of friends, the Firth family of Kipping House were prominent (see walk 6). It is possibly also significant that two local girls, Nancy and Sarah Garrs, who helped as housemaids, were happy to move with the family to Haworth in 1820.

The first indications of the Brontës as a literary family started with Patrick during this period. Two books by him, *The Cottage in the Woods* and *The Maid of Killarney*, were published in 1815 and 1818 respectively.

The Old Bell Chapel at Thornton is also included in this walk. For a description, see walk 6.

8. OXENHOPE AND HAWORTH

Haworth is the undisputed focal point of Brontë interest and tourism. The family home for many years, the Parsonage, stands close to the church and to the top of the steeply sloping main street, with the tourist information centre close by. The cobbled street is extremely picturesque, lined with cafés and individual shops.

Oxenhope has very much less Brontë association; formerly a village dominated by textile mills, it is probably now best known as the terminus of the Keighley and Worth Valley Railway, a preserved line with extensive collections of railway material and an excellent service of steam-hauled trains.

This walk uses the Brontë Way (see walk 3) as a route from Oxenhope to Haworth, with the return along a valley bottom path, close to the railway and to Bridgehouse Beck. The paths are mostly very good and not difficult to follow. Ascent is modest and there are very few stiles. Views from the high ground on the outward section are extensive.

DISTANCE	5.5km (3½ miles)
ASCENT	80m (263ft)
START/PARKING	Oxenhope railway station, grid reference 032354.
REFRESHMENTS	Oxenhope railway station (when the railway is operational); many inns and cafés in Haworth.
MAP	Ordnance Survey Explorer OL21, South Pennines, 1:25,000.

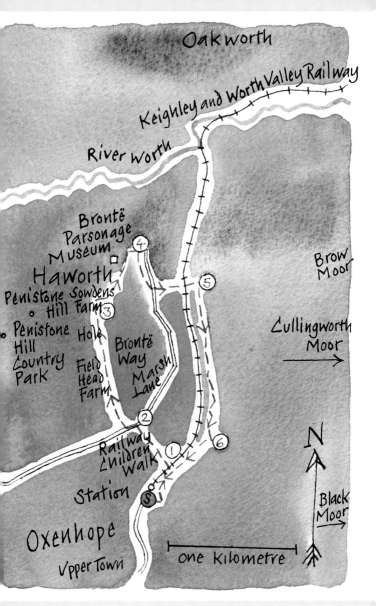

Oakworth

Keighley and Worth Valley Railway

River Worth

Brontë
Parsonage
Museum

Haworth

Penistone Sowdens
Hill Farm

Penistone
Hill
Country
Park

Hole

Field
Head
Farm

Brontë
Way

Marsh
Lane

Brow
Moor

Cullingworth
Moor

Railway
Children
Walk

Station

Oxenhope

Upper Town

N

Black
Moor

one kilometre

④

⑤

③

②

①

⑥

Ⓢ

THE WALK

(S) From the parking area by the station, walk back to a road junction. Turn left along a minor road (Mill Lane) to cross Bridgehouse Beck. Bear left at a public bridleway sign; the roadway soon becomes a path along the side of the beck, with railway sheds to the left. Go left to cross the beck on a footbridge.

(1) Go up to the left at a stile, cross the railway and then go up a few steps to another stile. Follow the obvious path rising along the edge of a field to reach Bents House (of the Railway Children film) at the top. Continue, left and then right, soon reaching tarmac at Marsh Lane.

(2) Turn left for 80m, pass Marshlands, and then turn right to follow Old Oxenhope Lane, still rising gently, to Field Head Farm. Immediately after the farm, turn right at a public footpath signpost, bearing left after a further few metres at another footpath sign. Keep a stone wall on the left as the path keeps close to the edge of a field, rising gently. There are extensive views across the valley, including a solitary wind turbine. When confronted by two gateways ahead, take that on the left, maintaining the same line. The wall is now on the right. There are signposts and little gates as the path passes above the hamlet of Hole. Go almost straight across a lane; there is a 'Haworth Main Street 775m' sign.

(3) Go right at a little gate to start the descent to Haworth along a walled footpath. Go straight ahead at a junction, passing a car park on the right. The path becomes paved before you reach the churchyard of Haworth Church and then the main street, with the tourist information centre to the left and the Black Bull on the right.

(4) Turn right to walk down the street. At the bottom cross the road junction, bearing left to continue the descent, with Central Park on the left. Cross the railway line. At a road junction turn right.

⑤ As Brow Road climbs steeply to the left, turn right at a 'Public Footpath to Oxenhope' sign. Go up a few steps to follow a clear path, through a kissing gate and past a signpost with multiple waymarks. The route stays generally in the valley bottom, never far from the beck and the railway. Cross a gated bridge and pass through a wooded section; keep left at a waymarked fork, and then right by a derelict dwelling, up to a stile. Pass in front of a house.

⑥ Just past the house turn right to follow a path descending back towards the beck. Continue beside the water. Pass but do not cross an attractive little bridge. Cross a more utilitarian bridge, go through a squeezer stile and stay by the beck. Cross the beck on a footbridge, with a millpond to the right. Pass a substantial dwelling, and then a water treatment works. After the works go through a waymarked kissing gate on the right to take a path leading directly to point 1 on the outward route. Return to the car park.

Previous pages: Haworth village.
Above: Main Street, Haworth.

Street between the Parsonage and the old school, Haworth.

At the Haworth end of this walk we are in Brontë heartland. The family's tedious removal journey in April 1820 (allegedly using seven farm carts and a light covered wagon) from Thornton culminated in the laborious ascent of the main street, as Mrs Gaskell described:

> The flag stones with which it is paved are placed end-ways, in order to give a better hold to the horses' feet; and, even with this help, they seem to be in constant danger of slipping backwards. The old stone houses are high compared to the width of the street, which makes an abrupt turn before reaching the more level ground at the head of the village, so that the steep aspect of the place, in one part, is almost like that of a wall. But this surmounted, the church lies a little off the main road on the left; a hundred yards, or so, and the driver relaxes his care, and the horse breathes more easily, as they pass into the quiet little by-street that leads to

Haworth Parsonage. The churchyard is on one side of this lane, the school-house and the sexton's dwelling (where the curates formerly lodged) on the other. (Mrs Gaskell, *Life of Charlotte Brontë*, chapter 1)

A short distance above the parish church, separated by part of the graveyard, is the Parsonage, built in 1779. Members of the Brontë family occupied this from 1820 to 1861. The symmetrical Georgian building of modest dimensions was distorted by the addition of a wing on the right gable in 1872 by Patrick Brontë's successor. In the twentieth century, the Brontë Society made extensions at the rear.

Since its acquisition by the Brontë Society in 1928, the Parsonage has become a museum, totally dedicated to the life and work of the Brontës, a great shrine to genius and to overwhelming sadness. Much of what is displayed is authentic Brontë furniture and possessions; likewise, the garden is apparently little changed. Note the statue of the three sisters in the garden behind the house. Overall, this modest property provides a definitive and inspirational Brontë experience for great numbers of visitors from all over the world.

Of the church (St Michael and All Angels) in which Patrick conducted services and the rest of the family worshipped, only the tower remains. Patrick's successor, the Revd John Wade, carried out 'restorations' (virtually a rebuild) in 1872. The new church is considerably bigger than the old and has a 'Victorian Gothic' appearance. Internally, the old box pews and three-decker pulpit of Patrick's day were cleared out. In 1964, the Brontë Memorial Chapel was added, furnished with objects that the Brontës would have known. The wedding register is displayed

Sign at the Parsonage, Haworth.

Apothecary's shop, Haworth.

and there is a tablet concerning the vault in which rest the remains of all the family except Anne, who is buried at Scarborough.

Across the lane from the churchyard is the building in which Charlotte taught on Sundays; an attempt by Charlotte, Emily and Anne to establish a day school here was unsuccessful. Below the school building are the sexton's house and the curate's lodgings.

By the nineteenth century the churchyard was already regarded as overfull, the horizontal slabs of the tombstones virtually edge to edge. It was recognized that the proximity of these crowded graves on high ground to the inadequate water supplies and drains on lower ground was a major factor in making Haworth one of the least healthy villages in the area. As part of the nationwide public health movement of the mid-nineteenth century, in 1850 the sanitary condition of Haworth was examined by an inspector, B. H. Babbage, on behalf of the General Board of Health. He found and reported on the horrendous water and drainage arrangements, which were largely responsible for a life expectancy of 25.8 years, comparable with some of the least healthy parts of London.

The graves of the Brontës' two long-serving servants, Tabitha (Tabby) Aykroyd and Martha Brown, can be seen close to the Parsonage garden wall.

Connecting the Parsonage with the churchyard and church was a little gate through the Parsonage garden wall (now blocked, but with a tablet) through which seven members of the family were carried on their final journey to the family vault.

At the top end of Main Street, facing one another, the Old Apothecary's Shop and the (since enlarged) Black Bull Inn are particularly associated with Branwell Brontë. At one he bought opium and at the other he comforted himself with alcohol, while enjoying social contact, both casual and at meetings of the local lodge of the Freemasons.

Joseph Brett Grant, a former curate of Patrick Brontë, became the first vicar at Oxenhope. In her novel *Shirley*, Charlotte based her character Revd Donne on Grant.

Plaque on the Brontë family vault at Haworth Parish Church.

9. PENISTONE HILL

This walk is focused on the upper part of the village of Haworth, where the combination of church, former Parsonage and school forms the nucleus of the Brontë presence which has transformed Haworth into a major visitor destination. For a description of Haworth, see walk 8.

Penistone Hill separates Haworth from the great and wild expanse of Haworth Moor. Now a country park, the hill itself comprises very accessible moorland, criss-crossed by numerous paths and scarred by extensive former quarrying activity.

This short and very easy walk provides a small sample of the landscape which is typical of the Pennine Moors.

DISTANCE	3.5km (2¼ miles)
ASCENT	50m (164ft)
START/PARKING	Pay-and-display car park close to the Parsonage, grid reference 029372.
REFRESHMENTS	Inns and cafés in Haworth, including the Black Bull, Branwell Brontë's favoured place of refreshment.
MAP	Ordnance Survey Explorer OL21, South Pennines, 1:25,000.

N

one kilometre

Oakworth

Keighley and Worth Valley Railway

ower
aithe
eservoir

Brontë
Parsonage
Museum

S Station

① Station

Haworth
Brow

Penistone Hill ③ ②

HAWORTH

Brow
Moor →

Penistone Hill
Country Park ④

onté
Vay

⑤

Quarries
(disused)

Brontë
Way

illennium
Way

laworth
Moor

Drop
Farm

Station

Oxenhope

Stanbury village.

THE WALK

ⓢ From the car park head towards the Parsonage (the Brontë Parsonage Museum), up a short ramp. Turn left at the top and walk for a few metres down a cobbled lane, passing the entrance to the Parsonage.

① Turn right through an old kissing gate above the church to take a path through the crowded churchyard; on the right is a plaque about the Brontë graves. At the far edge of the churchyard join another track. Turn right, soon leaving the

churchyard through another old kissing gate, to follow a flagged path, rising gently with allotments and chicken pens below to the left and long views across the Worth Valley. Pass a car park on the left to reach a signposted junction; go right towards 'Top Withens and the Brontë Falls', following a broad, rising track (Balcony Lane). Pass former farm buildings before reaching a public road.

② Cross the road to take a well-used footpath bearing left into Penistone Country Park (there is a sign on a rock).

③ At a fork in less than 400m go left towards the highest part of the hill. There is a signpost and also a plank bridge at the junction. At the top go across a more major path to reach the now disused triangulation point.

④ Continue straight ahead along a minor footpath. Join a better path and keep left around the top of former quarry workings. Bear right, passing a signpost and the pavilion of a cricket club. Go through a large car parking area and, as the unsurfaced access road leaves the left corner of this area, look carefully for a minor path on the right, starting between boulders. Follow this little path round the curve of a hillock, soon descending through an area with a few young trees.

⑤ Join a more major path, turning right to head back towards Haworth. Rejoin the outward route at point 3 and retrace the outward route back to the car park.

Lower Laithe Reservoir, Stanbury village and Haworth Moor from Penistone Hill.

The Parsonage at Haworth was home to members of the Brontë family for many years from their arrival in April 1820 until the death of Patrick in 1861. Following the foundation of the Brontë Society in 1893, the Parsonage eventually became the Brontë Parsonage Museum in 1928, a treasure house of Brontë memorabilia and a shrine for large numbers of Brontë enthusiasts from all over the world.

St Michael and All Angels Church sits immediately below the Parsonage. It is not where Patrick officiated and the family worshipped. A rebuild commissioned by Patrick's successor in the 1870s left only the bell tower from the earlier (smaller) building. There is, however, a Brontë chapel, completed in 1964, within the church and a plaque defining the position of the vault where members of the family are interred.

The moorland of Penistone Hill reaches close to the rear of the Parsonage. The Brontë sisters loved the moors, relishing the freedom to roam at will across these wide expanses in all seasons, deeply conscious of the wildness, the weather, the birds and the plants, all of which contributed to the unique atmosphere of the novels. In Emily's *Wuthering Heights*, in particular, the moor is an all-pervasive presence, at least as important as the human characters. She describes Linton's 'most perfect idea of heaven's happiness' as

The Parsonage, Haworth.

Track on Haworth Moor.

> . . . lying from morning till evening on a bank of heath in the middle of the moors, with the bees humming dreamily about among the bloom, and the larks singing high up overhead, and the blue sky and bright sun shining steadily and cloudlessly. (*Wuthering Heights*, chapter 24)

Although Emily was the Brontë sister most influenced by the character of the wild expanse, there is no doubt that her sisters also relished the freedom afforded by the ability to wander unconstrained in these wild places, almost literally at their back door.

For Charlotte the desolate moor provided the setting for Jane's grief-stricken flight from Thornfield after her parting from Mr Rochester in *Jane Eyre*. After leaving the coach at Whitecross Jane sets out across the moor, following the line of a stream until she comes to a craggy rock, leaning out of the ground. She sits down beneath the rock, the heather and mossy grass dry and still warm from the heat of the afternoon. As she is hungry, she gathers bilberries and drinks water from the stream. Then she lies down on the springy heather, with a grassy tussock for a pillow, spreading her shawl over herself, folded in two. After weeping for a while and saying a prayer, she curls up in her nest of moss and heather and falls into a deep sleep.

10. EAST RIDDLESDEN

A seventeenth-century manor house just outside Keighley, East Riddlesden Hall is a popular visitor attraction with a tea room and shop, owned and managed by the National Trust. The attractive property is set in formal and wild gardens, with a large pond.

The walk ascends through the suburban area of Riddlesden before crossing the farmland of the upper slopes of the valley of the River Aire, overlooking Keighley, with extensive views. The final section is along the towpath of the Leeds and Liverpool Canal. Most of the paths are reasonable but there are several stiles. The long ascent from the canal is all at an easy gradient. In one or two of the farms route-finding needs care.

East Riddlesden Hall.

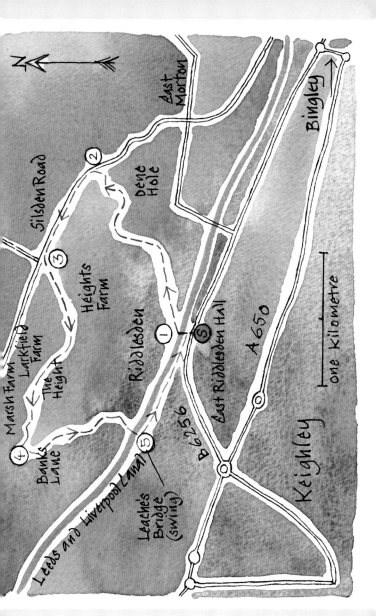

The Leeds and Liverpool Canal at Low Wood,
Riddlesden, overlooking Keighley.

DISTANCE	7.25km (4½ miles)
ASCENT	200m (656ft)
START/PARKING	Car parks at East Riddlesden Hall (National Trust), grid reference 080421.
REFRESHMENTS	Café at East Riddlesden Hall; Marquis of Granby Inn.
MAP	Ordnance Survey Explorer OL27, Lower Wharfedale and Washburn Valley, 1:25,000.

THE WALK

Ⓢ From the car park walk back to the main road. Cross at the pedestrian traffic lights and go up the road opposite, to the swing bridge over the canal.

① Cross the bridge; turn right at the Marquis of Granby Inn to follow Hospital Road, rising steadily through suburban Riddlesden. By the entrance to a long-defunct hospital go ahead along a signposted footpath, with a wall on the right. In approximately 200m, after crossing a modern estate road, turn left through an old stile and cross the estate road to go up through the estate, past Herdwick View, to a stile at the top. After another stile the path, now rural, continues to rise, close to How Beck, on the right. Continue, through gates/stiles, before bearing right to walk across the front of a row of cottages. At a road junction in 50m turn left, uphill, to follow a little road as far as the junction with a more important road at the top.

② Turn left to walk along the roadside verge. The views over the Aire Valley, with Keighley prominent, are extensive.

③ Turn left at a crossroads, signposted to Riddlesden. To the left is a holiday park. Stay with the road, passing a row of cottages and a farm. As the road dips to the left, go ahead at a stile/gate with a 'footpath' sign to take a broad, unsurfaced track passing behind a substantial dwelling, part of which is obviously very old. At the next buildings go right and then left, through squeezer stiles, to pass. Go along the bottom edge of a meadow. After the next farm buildings bear right along the edge of a field; the path rises slightly. At the next farm, the Height, the route needs extra care. Go through a gate, bear right and then turn left along the internal roadway. 20m after the left bend turn left; there is a little track leading to an old gate. Go through and head across a meadow to the next farm, Larkfield Farm. Go through a little gate and continue along the farm access roadway to join a public highway.

④ Turn left for a steady descent along the side of this very quiet road, still enjoying widespread views. On reaching the fringe of Riddlesden, the road descends more steeply. At the junction with Western Avenue look out for a signposted footpath, descending steeply, with steps, between the gardens of houses. Join a road at the bottom, turning right, downhill. This is Slade Lane. Descend to a road junction; go across this to Scott Lane West, bearing right. In 40m turn left into Leach Road, descending to reach a swing footbridge over the canal in approximately 200m.

⑤ Cross and turn left to walk along the towpath as far as point 1 of the outward route (approximately 0.8km). Turn right to cross the main road and return to the car park.

East Riddlesden Hall is one of the properties believed to have influenced Emily Brontë in her description of Thrushcross Grange, home of the Linton family in *Wuthering Heights*. Many regard it as the definitive model for that house, relocated near the edge of Haworth Moor (on the site of the present Ponden Hall?) in her story. East Riddlesden Hall was used for the exterior shots in the ITV adaptation of *Wuthering Heights* some years ago.

Alternatively (or additionally), the hall could have been in the mind of her sister Charlotte, for it fits her description of Mr Rochester's house, Thornfield, in *Jane Eyre*, when Jane says:

East Riddlesden Hall.

. . . advancing on to the lawn, I looked up and surveyed the front of the mansion. It was three stories high, of proportions not vast though considerable; a gentleman's manor house, not a nobleman's seat: battlements round the top gave it a picturesque look. Its grey front stood out well from the background of a rookery, whose cawing tenants were not on the wing. (*Jane Eyre*, chapter 11)

11. PONDEN RESERVOIR AND PONDEN HALL

Ponden Reservoir was created in the 1870s to enhance local water supplies. It is a pleasant sheet of water, used for recreational purposes. Ponden Hall is a very old farmstead, overlooking the reservoir.

This circuit is mainly across wild moorland, well above any cultivated areas. The tracks are mostly good and there are signposts and waymarks. However, there are narrow and rough sections requiring more than the usual care. The path passes over the top of the crag known as Ponden Kirk. The long initial ascent is at a reasonable gradient. Part of the route uses the Brontë Way.

DISTANCE	5.5km (3½ miles)
ASCENT	150m (492ft)
START/PARKING	Ample parking by the side of the minor cul-de-sac road on the south side of Ponden Reservoir, grid reference 995370. From the Haworth–Colne road turn left, either across the reservoir dam or along a very minor lane behind the former Ponden Mill, a little more than 1.6km (1 mile) west of Stanbury.
REFRESHMENTS	None en route.
MAPS	Ordnance Survey Explorer OL21, South Pennines, 1:25,000.

Ponden Hall and Reservoir.

THE WALK

Ⓢ Facing the water, turn left to walk along the road towards the west end of the reservoir. Keep right at a junction, going up past a guest house and Ponden Hall.

① Approximately 150m after passing the hall turn left at a junction towards Ponden Kirk, still ascending steadily. There are accumulations of derelict farm machinery beside the track. As the roadway goes left to a farm, keep straight ahead, along a signposted lane, to reach a gate and stile. A broad track now goes up across the moor. Pass a signpost; at a second signpost turn left to continue the ascent on a more minor track, heading for a gap in a wall above a farm.

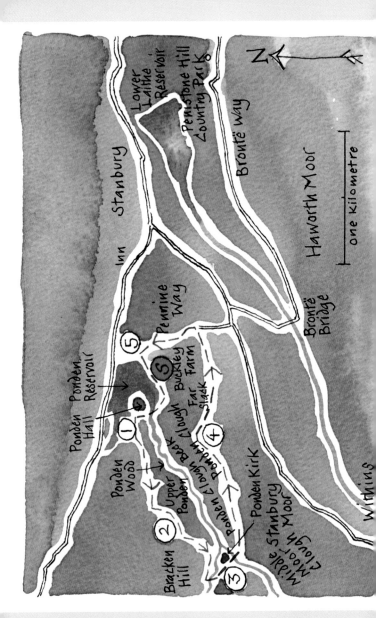

② Before the gap, turn right at a signpost to continue uphill, with a wall on the left. On reaching the top of the hill continue along a clear moorland path before turning left to descend to the (easy) crossing point of Ponden Clough Beck. The track goes to the left, keeping close to the rim of the steep-sided valley and passing above Ponden Kirk.

③ At the crossing of the next stream, with a bridge, there is a junction. (A left turn here is the start of a lower path which connects back to point 2. This makes a shorter circuit, permitting a better view of Ponden Kirk.) There is a 'Buckley Green and Stanbury' signpost. Follow this. The narrow path, clear between the moorland heather, descends gently towards Far Slack Farm. At a signposted junction go straight ahead, ignoring a ladder stile to the left. Go through a waymarked kissing gate above the farm buildings, joining a farm roadway in a few metres.

④ Turn right to walk along the farm roadway. Pass a signpost before reaching Buckley Green hamlet. Turn sharp left at the hamlet to go down an unsurfaced road towards Buckley Farm. By the farm entrance turn right, through a kissing gate with a 'Brontë Way' signpost, to descend along a broad path.

⑤ Join a surfaced road, close to the reservoir dam, and turn left to return to the parking area.

There has long been a widely held belief that the present Ponden Hall is the site of Thrushcross Grange, home of the Lintons in Emily Brontë's *Wuthering Heights*, which she describes as

> . . . a splendid place carpeted with crimson, and crimson–covered chairs and tables, and a pure white ceiling bordered by gold, a shower of glass drops hanging in silver chains from the centre, and shimmering with little soft tapers. (*Wuthering Heights*, chapter 6)

The house described by Emily appears to be larger and more imposing than Ponden Hall. Of the various theories concerning its inspiration, the site of Ponden Hall, bearing in mind that the present reservoir below the house did not then exist, is reasonably credible. Ponden Kirk, on the hillside overlooking Ponden Clough, is the most dramatic crag face in this extensive area of moorland. It was familiar to the Brontës, featuring as Penistone Crag in *Wuthering Heights*.

> 'Ellen, how long will it be before I can walk to the top of those hills? I wonder what lies on the other side – is it the sea?'
>
> 'No, Miss Cathy,' I would answer, 'it is hills again just like these.'
>
> 'And what are those golden rocks like, when you stand under them?' she once asked.
>
> The abrupt descent of Penistone Crags particularly attracted her notice, especially when the setting sun shone on it, and the topmost heights; and the whole extent of landscape besides

lay in shadow. I explained that they were bare masses of stone, with hardly enough earth in their clefts to nourish a stunted tree.

'And why are they bright so long after it is evening here?' she pursued.

'Because they are a great deal higher up than we are,' replied I; 'you could not climb them, they are too high and steep. In winter the frost is always there before it comes to us; and deep into summer, I have found snow under the black hollow on the north-east side.' (*Wuthering Heights*, chapter 18)

Stanbury village.

12. TOP WITHENS AND THE BRONTË BRIDGE

Haworth Moor is a large expanse of moorland which, merging with other similar moors such as Oxenhope Moor and Stanbury Moor, occupies much of the high ground between the former industrial areas of West Yorkshire and East Lancashire. Around the fringes of this harsh, windswept, heather-dominated landscape is marginal agriculture. The moor has long been a popular walking area and is traversed by footpaths, including the Brontë Way and the Pennine Way.

Reservoirs such as Ponden and Leeshaw were municipal constructions of the nineteenth century, meeting the need for abundant water for the fast-growing industries and populations of the nearby towns.

This walk is largely circular, visiting some of the most important and attractive features. Although the moor can be a desolate place, particularly in winter, the paths are easy to follow and well signposted. There are two stiles and also short lengths of rough, stony path either side of the Brontë Bridge. The aggregate ascent largely comprises two sections: first by Harbour Lodge Farm and second the approach to Top Withens.

Above: ruined wall, Haworth Moor.
Right: South Dean Beck, near Brontë Bridge.

DISTANCE	9.5km (6 miles)
ASCENT	198m (650ft)
START/PARKING	A small area beside a public convenience block on Moorside Lane (one of the many parking areas on the fringe of Penistone Hill), a little more than 0.8km (½ mile) south-west of Haworth, grid reference 019361.
REFRESHMENTS	Drop Farm, approximately 400m from the start of the walk (restricted opening hours); Haworth, with abundant inns and cafés, is a short drive (or walk) away.
MAP	Ordnance Survey Explorer OL21, South Pennines, 1:25,000.

THE WALK

Ⓢ Cross the public road and set off along an unsurfaced roadway (not the signposted road to Drop Farm), heading straight across Howarth Moor. Pass Drop Farm, to the left, and then pass well above Leeshaw Reservoir. As the track bends a little, Harbour Lodge Farm stands lonely ahead. Go up towards the farm.

① About 200m before the buildings turn right at a 'Top Withens' signpost, cross a little bridge over a stream and turn left at another signpost in a few metres. The path is now a rough moorland track, rising steadily past the farm. Go straight ahead at the next signpost to continue along

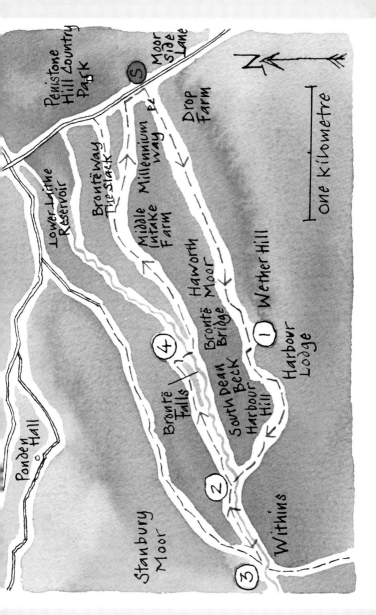

a narrow path high on the side of a valley. Descend steeply to a confluence of streams. Cross, bear left, and walk up to join a major track at a signpost.

② Turn left; Top Withens is now in view. Much of the path is now paved. Cross a stream on stepping stones before continuing the ascent to a junction with a 'Top Withens 200 yards' signpost. Turn left to reach a ruined farmhouse.

③ Return to the signpost at point 2, going straight ahead towards Brontë Bridge and Brontë Falls. Cross a wall on a ladder stile, pass through a squeezer stile and bear right to walk on a steep rough path down the valley side to the Brontë Bridge and nearby Brontë Falls (the latter need heavy rain to make any real impression).

④ Cross the bridge. Turn left to negotiate a rough section of path ascending towards Howarth. The route continues unmistakably, passing above the ruins of Far Intake Farm, and then by the side of the also ruined Middle Intake Farm. A short distance after this ruin, fork right along a minor footpath (Millennium Way) which rises gently across moorland to reach the minor road, Moorside Lane, opposite a parking area. Turn right at the public conveniences to walk back to the parking area.

Crossing the moor near Top Withens.

Ruined wall, Haworth Moor.

'Wuthering' being a significant provincial adjective, descriptive of the atmospheric tumult to which its station is exposed in stormy weather. Pure, bracing ventilation they must have up there at all times, indeed; one may guess the power of the north wind, blowing over the edge, by the excessive slant of a few stunted firs at the end of the house; and by a range of gaunt thorns all stretching their limbs one way, as if craving alms of the sun. Happily, the architect had foresight to build it strong: the narrow windows are deeply set in the wall, and the corners defended with large jutting stones. (*Wuthering Heights*, chapter 1)

Haworth Moor is unquestionably at the heart of Brontë Country. Able to walk to and from the moor directly from the Parsonage, Charlotte, Emily, Anne and occasionally Branwell spent a great deal of time happily wandering and exploring it at all times of year, with great influence on their subsequent writing. Charlotte recalled:

Ruined farm, Haworth Moor.

'My sister Emily loved the moors. Flowers brighter than the rose bloomed in the blackest of the heath for her; out of a sudden hollow in a livid hillside, her mind could make an Eden. She found in the bleak solitude many and dear delights; and not least and best-loved was – liberty. Liberty was the breath of Emily's nostrils; without it she perished.' (Elizabeth Gaskell, *Life of Charlotte Brontë*, chapter 8)

In Emily's *Wuthering Heights*, in particular, the moor becomes more than a mere passive background for the highly dramatic story; totally consistent with the untamed Heathcliffe and Cathy, it shares the impact which these personalities make on the reader.

Like Haworth, for Brontë enthusiasts Top Withens has, for many years, been a place of pilgrimage, to be visited almost with reverence. Situated high on the brow of the moor and reached only on foot, this ruined former farmhouse is regarded as occupying the site of Wuthering Heights. It is certainly not Wuthering Heights itself,

Rock outcrop near Brontë Bridge.

Top Withens.

as is emphasized by a plaque affixed to the building; Emily describes a larger, more imposing house. Sadly, Top Withens is not now even a romantic ruin; obviously in view of the large number of visitors, including children, it has been 'made safe' by removing the remains of the roof and much of the upper parts of the walls, resulting in a squat, truncated appearance.

Another focal point on the moor is at the confluence of South

Dean Beck and a small tributary stream, where the primitive Brontë Bridge crosses the beck and the tributary descends in a series of small falls – the Brontë Falls. Near by is a rock referred to as the Brontë Chair. As do many of today's visitors, the sisters lingered long in this relatively sheltered spot, sitting on stones, often part way across the stream. The capstone of the bridge is not the original; this was replaced after the bridge was damaged by floodwater.

13. WYCOLLER COUNTRY PARK

Wycoller Country Park is based on a charming hamlet discreetly tucked away in a valley on the Lancashire side of the Pennine Hills. Bisected by the Wycoller Beck, the hamlet has four bridges, including a superb two-arched packhorse bridge and an even older primitive clapper, the Clam Bridge. In the seventeenth and early eighteenth centuries Wycoller was

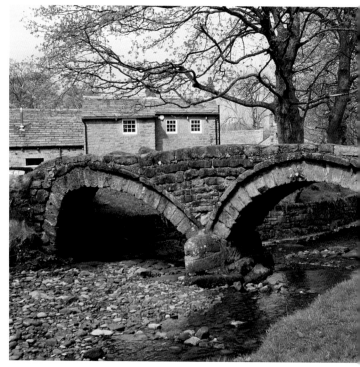

Packhorse bridge, Wycoller.

DISTANCE	2.5km (1½ miles)
ASCENT	10m (33ft)
START/PARKING	Official car park for Wycoller Country Park, approached from the direction of Laneshaw Bridge, grid reference 926395.
REFRESHMENTS	Café at Wycoller.
MAP	Ordnance Survey Explorer OL21, South Pennines, 1:25,000.

a thriving centre of handloom weaving but it was abandoned in the nineteenth century as the weaving industry became centralized in large mechanized mills in more accessible towns. The hamlet came back to life in the 1970s.

Wycoller Hall, now in ruins, was a sixteenth-century country house, much extended in 1774. A brief history is set out on an information board. Opposite the ruin is a great historic barn of structural significance, with a comprehensive internal display as a Countryside Information Centre. A pond, public conveniences and a shop/café add to the overall attraction of this delightful area.

This mini-walk is intended to familiarize the visitor with the features of Wycoller. It is entirely easy and without complication. The Brontë Way and the Pendle Way pass through the Country Park.

THE WALK

(S) At the car-park access road turn right to follow the hard-surfaced roadside footpath towards Wycoller village. There is a 'Wycoller village 500m' signpost.

(1) On reaching the village do not cross the stream. Continue on the nearside, passing the café/shop and the packhorse and clapper bridges. Bear right to follow a surfaced footpath through an area decorated with willow sculptures. At the far end of this area turn left to cross the stream on a more prosaic bridge.

(2) Turn left again to reach the information centre, housed in the historic barn (public conveniences are close by). Opposite the barn is the ruin of Wycoller Hall, with an information board. By the end of the packhorse bridge bear right, going up to another barn used as a study centre, with an overview of the hamlet. Bear left to rejoin the outward route and return to the car park.

Primitive clapper bridge, Wycoller.

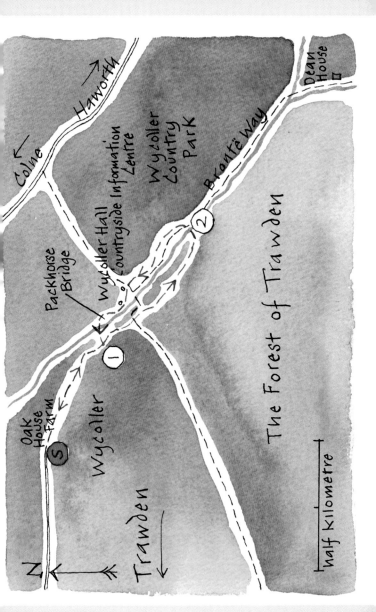

Haworth

Colne

Wycoller Hall Countryside Information Centre

Wycoller Country Park

Brontë Way

Dean House

Packhorse Bridge

①

②

Oak House Farm

S

Wycoller

Trawden

The Forest of Trawden

half kilometre

N

It has been suggested that the name Eyre, given to the principal character in Charlotte Brontë's *Jane Eyre*, was taken from Elizabeth Eyre, grandmother of Henry Owen Cunliffe, last squire of Wycoller. Clearly, Charlotte knew the area and also the history of the occupation of Wycoller Hall; see also walk 14. In her early writing she refers to a view of Boulsworth Hill, the substantial mound of

high moorland overlooking Trawden and the Wycoller Valley. The view is from Barnside, a farmstead a short distance to the north of the main Colne to Keighley road, east of Laneshaw Bridge. Wycoller is of sufficient importance for the Brontë Way to make a substantial diversion to the hamlet from the obvious direct route between Haworth and Gawthorpe Hall.

The ruins of Wycoller Hall.

14. TRAWDEN FOREST AND WYCOLLER

The Forest of Trawden is a large area of ancient hunting forest, surrounding the village of the same name.
It includes the modern Wycoller Country Park. The forest now largely comprises upland agriculture, mainly sheep farming, with some cattle. The extensive high moorland of Boulsworth Hill lies to the south.

Trawden is a former industrial village, typical of the late eighteenth and early nineteenth centuries, when textile barons were building their mills ever higher up the valleys on

both sides of the Pennines, utilizing the abundant water of the rushing streams for both power and processing. As the mills progressively closed in more recent times, Trawden lost its original purpose and it is now a rather nondescript village, strung along its only street.

Wycoller Country Park, with the remains of Wycoller village described in walk 13, is quite delightful and full of interest.

The high ground between Wycoller and Trawden is criss-crossed by field paths. Some of these are combined with a length of the Trawden road and a moorland section of the Brontë Way to give a well-varied and interesting circuit.

DISTANCE	10km (6¼ miles)
ASCENT	366m (1,201ft)
START/PARKING	Free Wycoller Country Park parking area by the side of the Colne/Laneshaw Bridge–Haworth road, high above Wycoller village, grid reference 937394.
REFRESHMENTS	Café at Wycoller; inn and café at Trawden (diversion).
MAP	Ordnance Survey Explorer OL 21, South Pennines, 1:25,000.

Trawden Forest, above Wycoller.

THE WALK

Ⓢ From the information boards in the parking area start down a few steps and a path leading to a little gate. Continue steadily downhill on a good path heading for the village at Wycoller. On the right is an example of the stone slab-on-end wall particular to this area. Near the bottom go left at a fork with a sign 'Aisled Barn'. Pass between the barn and public conveniences.

① Join a surfaced roadway. Turn right to pass the ruined Wycoller Hall, and soon turn left to cross Wycoller Beck on the ancient clapper bridge. Go ahead along a roadway rising up the valley side, with a tiny stream on the right. Leave the road up a waymarked flight of steps on the right. Go through a kissing gate into woodland, still ascending steadily. Go straight ahead at a junction to reach a stile at the top. To the left is Raven Rock Farm. After the stile continue the same line to a waymarked kissing gate. There is a wall on the left; Pendle Hill and part of Colne are now in view. After another stile, the north end of Trawden village comes into view. The next stile has a 'Brontës in Pendle, circular walk' waymark. The path continues straight ahead across upland sheep-grazing country. At Germany Farm go right to pass around the building. Cross a stream to a waymarked stile and continue to Little Laithe.

② Follow a narrow path between a wall and a hedge to a waymarked stile. Go over and commence the descent towards Trawden, now fully in view, generally on grass with a wall on the left. Go through a little gate to join a surfaced farm drive and continue down to Trawden. Cross a stream on a bridge and go up to join the village street. Most of the village, including refreshment, is to the right; visiting it requires an out-and-back deviation.

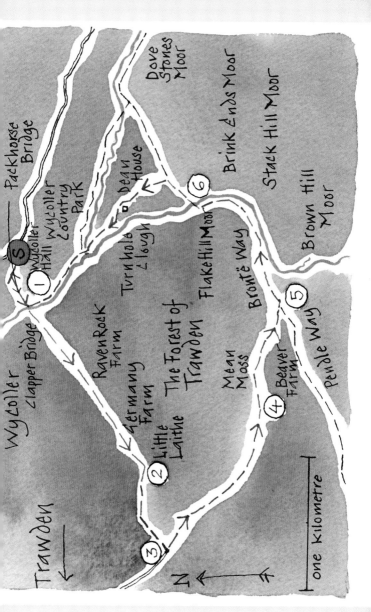

Traditional stone field boundary wall, above Wycoller.

③ To continue the circuit, turn left to walk along the roadside, soon leaving the village. The road (Boulsworth Road or Dark Lane) rises steadily, past a cul-de-sac sign. As it bends strongly to the left by a dwelling, go straight ahead along a broad track leading to a farm. At the farm, look for a gate on the left, with waymarks. Go through to go up across a huge field. There is no path; the route is to the right of diagonal, a little south of east. There is a gate/stile in the top right corner.

④ Join a farm access roadway, continuing towards the buildings of Mean Moss. After Mean Moss cross a cattle grid with 'Beaver Farm' signs. In 120m keep left at a fork. Ahead is Boulsworth Fell. The roadway continues; go straight ahead at a junction to reach a cattle grid, kissing gate and signposted junction.

⑤ Join the Pennine Bridleway (which is also the Brontë Way) and turn left. After an initial rise, the Way follows the edge of high moorland, and is almost level for some distance, with rough paving for much of the way and a deep clough on the right. Moorland birds are much in evidence. Descend to pass a post with multi waymarks, and a signpost a few metres further.

⑥ Turn right to cross the stream on a bridge, following a sign to 'Wycoller 1¾ miles'. The path rises initially to reach a signposted junction in approximately 400m. Turn left through a kissing gate with a 'Wycoller 1 mile' sign. There are two farms in view ahead. Aim for the left of the two, Dean House. There is no path across a huge descending meadow. Go to the right corner of a wall, bearing left to walk to the farm. Go through/over a waymarked gate/stile to pass through the farm and continue along the access drive. Join a very minor road (the meeting place of two sections of the Brontë Way), going ahead. Pass but do not cross a primitive bridge before reaching point 1 of the outward route. Turn right to return to the car park.

Primitive stile, Wycoller.

It is widely believed that Charlotte Brontë based Mr Rochester's home, Ferndean Manor, in *Jane Eyre* on Wycoller Hall. Mr Rochester moved to Ferndean Manor after his earlier, grander home, Thornfield, was destroyed by fire.

Even when within a very short distance of the manor house you could see nothing of it, so thick and dark grew the timber of the gloomy wood about it. Iron gates between granite pillars showed me where to enter, and passing through them, I found myself at once in the twilight of close-ranked trees. There was a grass-grown track descending the forest aisle between hoar and knotty shafts

and under branched arches. I followed it, expecting soon to reach the dwelling; but it stretched on and on, it wound far and farther: no sign of habitation or grounds was visible . . . I proceeded. At last my way opened, the trees thinned a little; presently I beheld a railing, then the house – scarce, by this dim light distinguishable from the trees, so dank and green were its decaying walls . . . The house presented two pointed gables in its front; the windows were latticed and narrow; the front door was narrow too, one step led up to it. The whole looked, as the host of the Rochester Arms had said, 'quite a desolate spot'. (*Jane Eyre*, chapter 37)

Ferndean Manor is described as uninhabited and unfurnished, which is what Wycoller Hall was in Charlotte's day. However, Charlotte's description of the surroundings, quoted above, is certainly not consistent with Wycoller Hall, which stood in the centre of a once busy little village.

It is probable that Charlotte, like her sister (see walk 12), drew on her experiences of different properties and places throughout the area, using selected features of those properties to arrive at her fictional homes and their locations.

Trawden Forest.

15. GAWTHORPE HALL

Very close to the built-up areas of Burnley and Padiham, Gawthorpe Hall stands in extensive grounds, largely wooded, in the broad valley of the River Calder. Managed by the National Trust, the hall is a considerable visitor attraction, with café, shop and adequate car parking.

This circuit uses Habergham Drive, a fine track rising through the grounds, and passes over higher ground on the Brontë Way before descending to the River Calder for a return along the Burnley Way.

Entirely good underfoot, with no difficult or steep ascents.

DISTANCE	7.5km (4¾ miles)
ASCENT	75m (246ft)
START/PARKING	Gawthorpe Hall car park, grid reference 806340.
REFRESHMENTS	Café at Gawthorpe Hall.
MAP	Ordnance Survey Explorer OL21, South Pennines, 1:25,000.

THE WALK

Ⓢ From the car park return to the entrance drive, turning left, towards the hall. Pass the entrance to the tea room.

① By the hall entrance gate turn sharp right, along a roadway rising through deciduous woodland; this is Habergham Drive and the final section of the Brontë Way. After a short distance go through a gate and keep straight ahead at a junction. Go straight ahead at a fork and leave the grounds of Gawthorpe Hall at a gate before joining a main road.

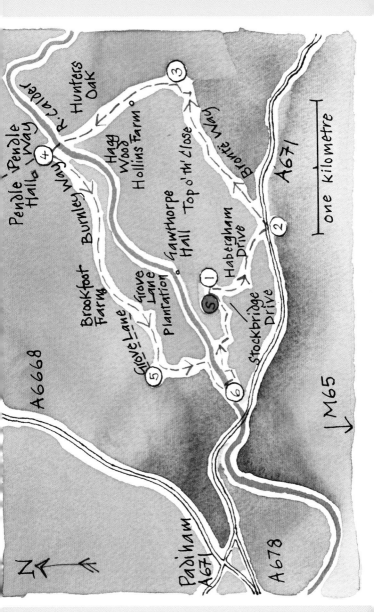

Gawthorpe Hall.

② Turn left to walk along the roadside footpath for 100m. At a 'public footpath, Cornfield Grove' sign turn left again, initially on a path between walls and soon with a school on the right. Continue to rise, going straight ahead to cross a minor road. The broad track (roadway) is partially hard surfaced, soon with a well-made footpath parallel on the right, which can be accessed by any one of three small gates. Join this excellent path and continue, with a modern housing development close on the right and Top o' th' Close Farm to the left. Reaching Manor House on the left, go ahead for 60m and then turn left along a housing estate road, staying with the main thoroughfare through the estate, as far as a T-junction.

③ Turn left, passing a cul-de-sac sign. The road soon becomes a pleasant country lane. Pass Pendle View Garden Centre, before beginning a long descent into the valley of the River Calder, with long views to the north, towards Pendle Hill (of witches fame). Ignore any tracks to the right or left. The surfaced lane ends by the gates to a large residence. Go ahead through a little gate to reach a waymarked gate and a footbridge over the river.

④ Over the bridge turn left and go through a gate marked 'Burnley Way', soon joining a hard-surfaced farm access drive. Continue along this drive, initially staying close to the river before passing the end of the drive to Hollins Farm and then Brookfoot Farm. As you reach the near end of Grove Lane Plantation, there is a choice: either stay with the roadway or go to the left immediately after crossing a bridge over a stream to follow a minor (and possibly muddy) path along the lower edge of the woodland. The routes rejoin at the far end of the wood, where there is an information board and a small parking area.

⑤ Go left to follow a concrete surfaced path, with grazing land on the left and soon with industrial/commercial buildings on the right. Reach the river, turning right to walk to the public road (Holmes Street). There are seats along the way. At Holmes Street turn left to cross the river on a footbridge.

⑥ After the bridge turn left immediately to follow a footpath heading into woodland. At a fork bear right, uphill. Stay with this clear path, ignoring paths to right and left, until it joins the Gawthorpe Hall entrance drive. Turn left to return to the car park.

Gawthorpe Hall has been the ancestral home of the Shuttleworth family for many centuries. Their original home at Gawthorpe (around 1300) is believed to have been a pele tower (a basic defensive small castle providing refuge from raiders from north of the Scottish border, more common in what is now Cumbria). By 1599 the family had prospered and the present house was constructed around the pele tower. The hall was modernized in the 1850s by Sir Charles Barry, architect of the Houses of Parliament, who gave it a more Elizabethan appearance.

In the nineteenth century the family name was changed to Kay-Shuttleworth when the heiress Janet Shuttleworth married Dr James Phillips Kay, who became a baronet in 1849. As Sir James Kay-Shuttleworth he became a notable benefactor of the poor and an advocate of a modern education system.

Sir James was a great admirer of Charlotte Brontë, on a number of occasions pressing her to visit him and his wife at Gawthorpe Hall. After he had visited the Brontës' home at Haworth, in March 1850 Charlotte agreed to go to Gawthorpe, and reputedly found it much to her taste. Later the same year she enjoyed more hospitality from the Kay-Shuttleworths, staying with them at their holiday home at Bowness in the Lake District, where she met Mrs Gaskell, her future biographer.

After Charlotte's marriage to her father's curate, Arthur Bell Nicholls, Sir James again visited Haworth, in order to offer the Revd Nicholls a living at Habergham, near Burnley.

Early in 1855, Charlotte, accompanied by her husband, made a final visit to Gawthorpe Hall. She was not in good health and her condition was apparently worsened by catching a chill after a morning walk over wet grass, wearing thin shoes. After returning to Haworth she died later in the year.

he garden at Gawthorpe Hall.

CHRONOLOGY

1777 Patrick Brunty (later Brontë) is born in County Down, Ireland.

1783 Maria Branwell (later Mrs Brontë) is born in Penzance, Cornwall.

1802–6 Patrick attends St John's College, Cambridge, and becomes a BA.

1806–9 Patrick is curate at Wethersfield in Essex, Wellington in Shropshire, and Dewsbury.

1811 Patrick is curate at Hartshead.

1812 Patrick and Maria meet at Woodhouse Grove School, Apperley Bridge. They marry at Guiseley at the end of the year.

1814 Maria Brontë is born at Hartshead.

1815 Elizabeth Brontë is born at Hartshead.

1815 Patrick becomes the incumbent at Thornton.

1816 Charlotte Brontë is born at Thornton.

1817 Patrick Branwell Brontë is born at Thornton.

1818 Emily Jane Brontë is born at Thornton.

1820 Anne Brontë is born at Thornton.

1820 Patrick Brontë becomes the incumbent at Haworth.

1821 (Mrs) Maria Brontë dies.

1823 Patrick Brontë's attempts at remarriage are unsuccessful.

1823 The late Mrs Brontë's unmarried sister Elizabeth, 'Aunt Branwell', moves from Cornwall to Haworth.

1824 Maria and Elizabeth go to Cowan Bridge School, and are followed by Charlotte and Emily.

1825 Maria and Elizabeth leave Cowan Bridge; both die of tuberculosis. Charlotte and Emily are brought home to Haworth.

1831 Charlotte goes to Miss Wooler's school at Roe Head. There she meets Ellen Nussey and Mary Taylor, who become lifelong friends.

1832 Charlotte leaves Roe Head.

1835 Charlotte returns to Roe Head as a teacher. Emily goes to Roe Head as a pupil, staying for only two months. Anne goes to Roe Head as a pupil, staying for two years. Branwell studies painting, intending to go to the Royal Academy in London. He later opens a studio in Bradford, but without success.

1837–41 Emily, Anne and Charlotte have a series of posts as governesses at Halifax, Mirfield, Lothersdale, Thorp Green and Rawdon.

1840 Branwell becomes a tutor at Broughton-in-Furness, Westmorland, for a short time. He becomes a railway clerk at Sowerby Bridge and then Luddenden Foot.

1842 Charlotte and Emily go to M. Heger's school in Brussels. Aunt Branwell dies. Charlotte and Emily return to Haworth. Branwell is dismissed by the railway company.

1843 Charlotte returns to Brussels for a year. Anne and Branwell both become tutors at Thorp Green.

1844 Revd Arthur Bell Nicholls becomes curate at Haworth.

1845 Anne leaves Thorp Green. Branwell is dismissed from Thorp Green in disgrace.

1846 Publication of *Poems* by Charlotte, Emily and Anne, under the assumed names of Currer, Ellis and Acton Bell. Emily's *Wuthering Heights* and Anne's *Agnes Grey* are accepted for publication. Charlotte's *The Professor* is rejected.

1847 Charlotte's *Jane Eyre* is published and is an immediate success. *Wuthering Heights* and *Agnes Grey* are also published but without success.

1848 Anne's *The Tenant of Wildfell Hall* is published. Branwell dies. Emily dies.

1849 Anne dies. Charlotte's *Shirley* is published.

1850 Charlotte visits Gawthorpe Hall (near Burnley), London, Edinburgh and Windermere. She meets Mrs Gaskell.

1851 Charlotte visits London again.

1852 Charlotte visits Filey and Scarborough (Anne's place of burial).

1853 Charlotte's *Villette* is published. Charlotte visits London and Manchester (spending a week with the Gaskells). Mrs Gaskell visits Haworth.

1854 Charlotte becomes engaged to and marries the curate Arthur Bell Nicholls. They spend their honeymoon in Ireland.

1855 On a winter visit to Gawthorpe Hall Charlotte catches cold and dies on 31 March.

1857 Mrs Gaskell's *Life of Charlotte Brontë* is published. Charlotte's *The Professor* is published.

1861 Patrick Brontë dies. Arthur Bell Nicholls returns to Ireland.

FURTHER READING

Starting with Elizabeth Gaskell's biography of Charlotte in the 1850s, there has been an enormous wealth of literature concerning every aspect of the Brontë family, their lives, their work and their environment. Of necessity in a book of walks, the list below is short and not all of the books mentioned are necessarily in print at the present time. For a comprehensive selection of books both new and second-hand, a visit to the shop managed by the Brontë Society at the rear of the Parsonage in Haworth is recommended.

There are numerous editions of the seven novels:
Anne Brontë, *Agnes Grey*, 1847
—, *The Tenant of Wildfell Hall*, 1848
Charlotte Brontë, *Jane Eyre*, 1847
—, *Shirley*, 1849
—, *Villette*, 1853
—, *The Professor*, 1857
Emily Brontë, *Wuthering Heights*, 1847
Shortened and simplified versions are available of *Jane Eyre* and *Wuthering Heights* (Usborne Classics, 2006), suitable for younger readers.

Juliet Barker, *The Brontës*, 1995
Ann Dinsdale, *The Brontës at Haworth*, 2006
Mrs Elizabeth Gaskell, *The Life of Charlotte Brontë*, published first in 1857 in two volumes, and subsequently in various editions
Lancashire County Planning Department, *The Brontë Way*, 1998
W. R. Mitchell, *Haworth and the Brontës*, 1981
Arthur Pollard, *The Landscape of the Brontës*, 1988

INDEX

(AB), (CB) and (EB) refer to Anne, Charlotte and Emily Brontë.

Page numbers in *italic* refer to illustrations.